Also by Dr. Bill

Wake Up! Wise Up! Win!

Back from the Valley of the Shadow of Death

Enjoy the Easy Life with Jesus

JERK-STORIES

Tales of Torture at the Office

Inflicted by
Managers Gone Wild

By
Dr. L. F. "Bill" Zimmermann

<u>Key Words</u>

Personal Assets
Personal Traits
Personal Values
Social Attitudes
Communication Skills
Employee Support
Organizing Skills
Directing Skills
Controlling Skills
Organizational Management
Employee Motivation (Psychology)
Leadership
Micromanagement
Harassment

Dedication

I dedicate this book to all those long-suffering employees subject to cruel and unusual pain inflicted by a multitude of jerk-managers.

Forward

As far as I know, *jerkism* is a word I coined describing the attributes of persons who make the world difficult for otherwise happy and productive people.

My own managerial effectiveness research, conducted over a fourteen-year period, involving almost 500 workers, from more than 200 different organizations, engaged in 43 different industry classifications, established a benchmark for how employees graded the effectiveness of their management. The average grade is only 68% out of 100%. To me, this certainly indicates that there are lots of jerk-managers out there managing all types of business.

This original research also produced a listing of 24 positive management and leadership traits most employees expect of their management.

Personal Traits
Creative Vision
Critical Thinking Ability
Good Ethics
Loyalty to Company and Workers
Personal Integrity
Reliability
Sufficiently Educated
Trustworthy and Trusting

<u>People Skills</u>
Acknowledges Good Work
Available to Workers
Effective Communication Skills
Exhibit Friendliness
Impartiality and Fairness
Personal Support for Workers
Respectability and Respect for Workers
Shows Interest in the Workers

<u>Management Skills</u>
Ability to Solve Problems
Accountability
Effective Decision Making Ability
Effective Follow-Up Efforts
Good General and Job Specific Knowledge
Impartial Evaluations
People and Organizational Skills
Provides Effective Training

The stories supporting this book consist of short accounts from working adults recounting what I call their *Jerk-Stories*. While this book is not a formal scientific research project in any way, over 100 working adults have volunteered their true–to-life histories.

I cannot assert that all of these stories used in this book are true. While the storytellers remain anonymous, they all claimed their stories are true and factual.

Nevertheless, for purposes of this book, we will assume they are all true. They surely sound true.

Although all of the participants told a similar story of pain imposed at the hands of a jerk-manager, only those that are were most common are included in this book. They all sound familiar and are typical of the jerk-managers I have personally known.

While there are specific *Jerk-Stories* in each chapter, each story could more than likely fit into any chapter.

Simply put, jerk-managers have unlikable personal traits, poor people skills, and very few management skills. It seems that most jerk-manager's problems cluster around a lack of personal values, anti-social attitudes and ineffective communication skills.

In fact, some of these *Jerk-Stories* might sound very familiar to a *jerk-story* of your own. I could recognize several of them from my own experiences with jerk-managers.

However, due to an effort to insure anonymity and to avoid any details that could link these stories to any actual parties involved, in each case we removed the names of jerk-managers, organizations and places. Not all of the stories are about individuals. Some of them are stories of jerk attitudes in general.

As prompted by my Spelling and Grammar check, the stories have only been modified for some minor typographical errors, grammatical errors, awkward sentences and spelling errors. I have also inserted some pronouns in place of actual names to maintain anonymity. In all cases, the original intent of the storytellers has not been changed.

DO
YOUR PART
HELP
ERADICATE
JERKISM.

Table of Contents

Chapter One

JERKISM

Defining Jerks

There is an old saying, "Nice guys finish last." I believe nothing could be farther from the truth. I think a better statement is "Jerk-managers never last."

Some jerks might seem to finish first. Some make lots of money and have fame and fortune, but they can also suffer from low self-esteem, often lose their families, lose their friends, and live miserable personal lives.

Actually, many often lose their jobs and fortunes too. My own experience in business tells me that most jerk-managers eventually get their comeuppance.

Nice people do not all become rich and famous. Be that as it may, nice people have nice families, nice friends, nice relationships, nice dispositions and they live nice contented lives. In the game of life, nice people finish happily.

I know I am opening myself up to possible harsh criticism from the ranks of academia and organizational management practitioners by using such a coarse term to define many of the people in business management today. Nevertheless, in my mind, there is no better word to describe them.

Some of the *Jerk-Stories* in this book are short and to the point, while some are long and detailed. Many of the storytellers sound as though they are still mad at the jerk who managed them. Most of the writers are over their past agony, but still have a detailed memory of the distant trauma.

Many of these *Jerk-Stories* end with the storyteller deciding to quit his or her job. Some of the stories tell of employees, who for one reason or another, have to continue to put up with the bad behavior of their bosses. Sadly, fear of losing one's livelihood is strong motivation for putting up with a jerk-manager.

In truth, some of the stories sound as though the storytellers might be somewhat jerky too. It is reasonable to consider that some employees contribute to the jerkiness of their managers.

Unfortunately, I too have observed and worked with several momentous jerk-managers. The experiences were not pleasant. Luckily, I was able to tell my jerk-managers goodbye and move on.

Perhaps, if you are a manager, the stories in this book will help you avoid catching the destructive disease of *jerkism*.

The list of 24 positive traits listed in the foreword gives us a litany of things that describe a good, effective leader-manager. These are the things that employees expect of their managers. Any argument based on reasonable logic can explain what each of these traits encompasses and why they are important.

During my many years in management, I have found that the rewards gained from employees' self-motivation and high morale directly relate to how managers meet their employees' social and self-esteem needs.

In the United States and Western Europe, managers do not usually have to deal with employees operating at Maslow's *survival* or *safety* needs levels (Maslow, 1954). Our employees are usually not starving and tend to feel safe at work. Of course, some jobs such as law enforcement workers, fire fighters and soldiers have physically risky jobs.

However, managers do have to be concerned about their employees' social and self-esteem needs. Managers who do not understand that their employees are human, and that their employees have the same basic human needs as they have are hell-bent for *jerkism*.

Unfortunately, we cannot simply tell someone to be trusting, dependable, ethical, and nice, and that he or she will succeed as a result. It is also impractical to think you can learn to be a good manager and leader simply from reading this book.

People have to recognize on their own how to be a nice person and good manager. They also need to understand why all of these good traits are important to success in life in general.

On the other hand, I think the *Jerk-Stories* in this book do give a clear picture of what a poor manager looks like, and what makes him or her fail at leadership.

Generally, people learn to be good managers in two ways, 1) working for good managers and emulating what those managers do and how they do it, and 2) learning to be good mangers by looking at what not to do and how not to do it.

I hope that looking at the way these employees viewed their managers will be of great value in helping would-be-leaders shun bad behavior, which can destroy an employee's self-motivation, kill organizational morale, and severely reduce potential peak-performance.

Admittedly, poor morale does not necessarily translate into creating unacceptable performance. In most cases, even unhappy employees still get their jobs done. However, we can never know how much better quality or increased productivity would result if those same employees were happy in their work environment.

I have never seen happy employees experience burnout on the job. Happy employees enjoy coming to work, enjoy their work, and enjoy the people and customers they work with at their jobs.

Nevertheless, burnout exists. I do know good people who have left an otherwise good job because of burnout. Most of them do not leave the job because it is hard work. They leave the job because of personal stress brought on by working in a hostile managerial environment.

I can tell you that I know this feeling first-hand. After four years in an otherwise great high-profile management job, I resigned because of a newly hired jerk-in-charge. The job itself was very rewarding, but the negative atmosphere became unbearable when this person took over.

At the time I resigned, two other department heads serving under this person resigned within two weeks. One department head resigned the week before me and the other quit the week after me.

Unfortunately, the organization lost a great deal of job knowledge and excellent performing employees due to that one jerk-manager.

After spending more than 40 years in various management positions, my fervent hope is that I have never been a jerk-manager myself. So far, I do not think I have been. At least no one has called me a jerk to my face.

Of course, like most others, I owe my personal traits, any people skills, and any managerial success that I have had to my family upbringing. My family taught me that the Golden Rule was the best motto to live by.

My father, John Antoni Zimmermann was my hero. He spent his entire adult life serving others. Everyone says my father was a very well-liked and respected man. I have never heard a bad word said about my father.

As State Director of Recreation for the WPA during the Great Depression in the 1930s, my father helped to make life exciting and fun for all of the children of Louisiana. I remember the great summer camps the WPA established throughout Louisiana and the numerous recreation programs for children and adults all year long.

Later, as Director of all of the USO clubs in seven southern states during WWII, my father helped to provide rest and recreation for thousands of men and women in the Armed Services. The USO clubs under his control provided entertainment, food, and lodging to all visiting troops in the armed services.

After WWII, he worked as a funds-raising professional. He headed funds-raising campaigns for organizations including, the United Way, the Heart Fund, the United Negro College Fund and many other local non-profit groups.

My father never made much money for himself. Yet, he reached every one of his funds-raising goals and raised millions of dollars for others.

The staffs of all of those funds-raising campaigns he managed were volunteer workers. You cannot be a jerk if you rely on volunteers.

I believe that my father was the way he was because he also grew up in an atmosphere of concern for others. He always told me about how his grandfather, Philip Antoni, helped care for the sick and dying during the yellow fever epidemic in New Orleans in the 1860s.

My great grandfather moved into the rectory of the Dominican priest and nursed his pastor, Blessed Fr. Francis X. Seelos, day and night during his last weeks on earth as he lay dying of yellow fever. Yet, my grandfather, who caught the fever himself, lived until 1909.

Nice people are not perfect. They are just nice to deal with in their imperfections. Perhaps being an Eagle Scout since I was 14 has also helped in my attempts at being a nice person.

I still believe in the Boy Scout Code of Honor and suggest that mangers take the same oath.

Trustworthy - Loyal - Helpful – Friendly - Courteous - Kind - Obedient – Cheerful - Thrifty - Brave - Clean and Reverent

Those twelve traits provide the basis for true success in life. They describe who you are. They give you a roadmap to self-confidence and high self-esteem. You do not have to be a Boy Scout to abide by this code of honor. However, if you steadfastly live by this code, I guarantee there is little chance that you will ever be a jerk.

Of course, we do have to acknowledge that there are also many jerk-employees. The reality is that jerk-employees exhibit the same kinds of traits as jerk-managers.

However, competent managers can usually handle jerk-employees with little worry. Competent mangers have sufficient self-esteem and self-confidence to understand that jerk-employees can only cause trouble if allowed to do so.

While at the same time, we must understand that the combination of a jerk-employee working for a jerk-manager is usually a volatile problem. Jerk-employees only get *jerkier* in response to jerk-management. They become more and more cynical, and engage in more and more bad behavior and bad-mouthing of the company.

Top management must recognize this destructive situation and take corrective action. Left alone, it will only get worse.

The following chapters are devoted to analyzing how jerk-mangers fail to fulfill the expectations of their subordinates. We can divide the three major categories of expectations into several sub-categories in each area.

Starting with personal traits, we subdivide them into the following two main sub-categories: 1) Personal Values, and 2) Personal Assets

As we go through these *Jerk-Stories*, you will undoubtedly see that most of the jerk-managers fail to deliver on almost each and every one of the employee expectations of management. Certainly, they fail to deliver on most of them.

At this point, it is important to say that although many jerk-managers are micro-managers, we should not classify all micro-managers are jerk-managers. There is a difference between nice people who micro-manage and jerk-managers. Conversely, all jerk-managers are not all micro-mangers. In fact, many of them do not manage at all.

I suggest that as you read these stories, put yourself in the position of the storytellers, and think about how you would feel in the same situation. My guess is that you would not feel very comfortable in their shoes.

In the following chapters, we will look at some of the many *Jerks-Stories* selected for this book. We will look at why the bad behavior is destructive, and maybe find some answers to preventing this type of behavior in the future.

Chapter Two

Personal Values

Experience tells us that the fundamental makeup of a manager's personal traits gives us a clue as to why so many are jerk-managers. We start with *Personal Values,* because I believe they form the foundation for most behavior.

Personal Values determine who we are and what we stand for. Personal Values include *personal integrity, trustworthy and trusting, good ethics, reliability, and loyalty to company and workers.*

From early childhood, most of us learn to trust or distrust certain people. Children of abusive parents learn fear, and they are always on guard that anyone can turn against them.

If children can recognize when adults are unreliable and disloyal, is it any wonder that adult workers will do likewise. Does it make sense that people would not want to work around people they cannot trust?

Instinctively, we do not trust unethical people who have little integrity. We see that they are not trustworthy, and we understand that they probably do not trust us either.

Regardless of our station in life, we only have our own ethics and moral principles to guide us in our relationship with others. If we do not trust others and are not loyal to others, how can we expect to receive trust and loyalty in return? I think most people would agree that ethics and integrity dictate that we never knowingly do harm to others.

These first stories in this chapter give us some insight into why jerk-mangers, who have questionable personal values, produce such adverse effects on their workers.

This story also hits home with me. As the saying goes, I have seen this situation up close and personal.

Episode # 1

We start with a common problem in the workplace. It is a simple, yet powerful saga. It brings up an all-important question. Do you think employees can trust a two-faced manager?

You know, I had a boss that would smile in your face and say bad things about you behind your back.

To his boss, he was a good manager. But, he did not have people skills.

That story reminds me of the reason why I resigned from the position I talked about earlier. The boss I had would try to play each of the department heads against each other. It led to three out of four of us resigning from our positions.

Along the same line, spreading false gossip is the quickest way to kill teamwork in any organization. Managers who talk behind their employees' backs simply cannot be trusted. They have no respect for their workers, and usually display favoritism in the organization. Most employees can easily spot a backbiter when the see one.

Actually, backbiting and gossip are two of the main deterrents to good communication. Managers do not have to tell everything to every employee, but what they do say must be the truth.

Victims of gossip will become wary of the people they work with. They wonder what the others have heard and said about them. They begin to avoid contact and conversation with those around them for fear of more negative gossip. They begin to feel ostracized and rejected.

Once negative gossip gets started, it is almost impossible to reverse it. In many cases, the victim of gossip ends up leaving the group.

Sneaky people fail completely at this basic personality aphorism:

Blessed are the pure in heart.

Episode # 2

The following *Jerk-Story* touches directly on personal integrity, being trustworthy and trusting, and good ethics. Greed is one of the most destructive forces contributing to the downfall of many people and organizations.

I've heard some terrible stories, though the most had to do with ever-changing compensation plans and slooooooow reimbursement for expenses.

One guy had over $10K on his personal charge card, because his boss was intentionally holding off paying him. Come to find out, it was because his boss was paid based on his P&L. So, while this guy was getting hit with double digit interests rates, his boss was collecting more commission.

Now that's a jerk!

This is an excellent example of greed, and of how it can cause dishonesty and resentment in the workplace. In addition to the fact that nobody likes someone messing with their money, this boss showed total disregard for his employees' well being.

Is there any question why the employees did not trust this jerk? This person was obviously not trustworthy or loyal.

I think we can admit that most people want to make more money. That is normal and actually a good thing for business. Moving up in an organization and receiving greater rewards for greater productivity is essential to good career advancement. On the other hand, advancement and making more money at the expense of those you work with is certainly unethical, if not illegal in some cases.

I believe that pitting one employee against the others is one of the dangers of intra-office incentive systems. When one person is sabotaging the efforts of the others, in order to come out on top, it will sometimes cause resentment and actually result in lower productivity

Episode # 3

This sad, but all too common tale, also tells of someone who has little integrity and cannot be trusted.

She has no ethics, is unreliable and is not loyal to anyone. This kind of supervisor makes life miserable. They are totally self-centered.

Why my manager was a Jerk! She was never there when you needed her. She was always on break, and would take other favored employees on break with her. She would come in on vacation for ten minutes, and then say she was not taking that day as a vacation day because she had to come in to work. But, she never really came in for work-related issues.

She would not stand up for her employees. She did not lead by example. She was more of a "do what I say, not what I do" kind of person. She thought that employees with degrees were not any more educated than the ones without a degree.

She would kiss up to whomever she thought had the power to help her. She had everyone else do her work, and then she would take credit for it. However, if the work was incorrect, she would have you to take the blame for it.

This is another case where a jerk-manager will step on anybody in order to get ahead. This jerk-manager suffers from low self-esteem, masked by an act of superiority. We also see that she falls short on all of the big three categories. She has few personal assets, she exhibits anti-social behavior, and she certainly lacks communication skills.

One of the most important things employees look for in a good job situation is recognition for a job well done. Taking credit for the storyteller's good work is a sure sign that the supervisor had no personal regard for this employee.

Going back to my list of tried and true maxims, these two fit this situation to a tee.

Blessed are the poor in spirit
and
Blessed those who hunger and thirst for justice

A better-than-thou attitude does not help a person to be poor in spirit. When we are poor in spirit, we know and understand that we all need other people in our lives.

Justice in the workplace calls for honesty in acknowledging and rewarding employees for their work. Jerk-managers who take all the credit for another's work show no regard for fairness and justice.

In social terms, narcissistic pride does not make friends or bring happiness. Bragging, bravado and bigotry are usually cover-ups of low-self esteem. Do you like having a conversation with a person who only talks about him or herself?

Episode # 4

While the person submitting the next story does not detail this jerk-manager's exact behavior, it follows that the lack of respect he gets from the employees stems from his lack of respect for himself. He also shows a lack of loyalty to the company and his employees.

I have worked for many managers in the past. However, I have worked for a person who micro-managed everyone in the office. He did not know how to motivate my co-workers or me.

Although, he managed the operation, he had very little respect as an authoritative figure. Whenever he managed the shift, most of my co-workers said they performed as little work as possible. My passion for the company went down the tubes because of this jerk.

This former boss had a classic case of Jerkism. I have promised myself. I will not be a Jerk whenever I manage people. Moreover, I will adopt the "Y" style of management, when I am in charge of individuals. If a manager is a jerk, he or she will not get the same amount of respect as a manager who is not a jerk.

A jerk manager will have one person perform meaningless task, which will result in poor production. Most employees perform at his or her best whenever management lets them perform on his or her own. I personally do not like it when my manager asks me about every decision I make on the job.

Most managers with a jerk style of leadership suffer from a lack of formal training and proper support. The result usually will be lower sales and production for the company.

Reading between the lines of the above story, we can easily determine that the writer insinuates that the jerk-manager has few personal assets as well as doubtful personal values, and even less people skills. The jerk-manager appears to have poor job knowledge, is not very creative, and has trouble thinking problems through.

This is a great example of how poor management can drastically lower productivity. Incompetent jerk-mangers deflate their workers normal self-motivation.

I agree with this writer that most people want to do a good job and want recognition as good workers. This manager is so hapless, he does not even recognize that his employees are purposely not being productive.

Although we have said that not all micro-managers are jerk-managers, this micro-manager is certainly a jerk. He acts out of very poor self-esteem and thinks that the people he manages are just as incapable as he is. Of course, these kinds of jerk-managers seldom realize how incapable they are.

Episode # 5

The following story illustrates a situation arising from outside pressures that cause a manager to behave badly on the job.

We can only understand the impact of this story by realizing that this manager was bringing his personal domestic problems to work with him. Managers who manage based on their emotions rather than good business practices usually have a problem with their efforts at achieving good employee relationships.

He was my supervisor on the first full time job I had. I worked as an administrative specialist in a local office in the country. All of my co-workers were Japanese locals. He was the only other American. On the first day of my work, some of the people in the other offices warned me about his mood swings.

I heard that my predecessor has chosen to (or was forced to) transfer out to another branch because he did not get along with him. First thing he asked me on the interview was "Do you cry?" He even told me straight to my face that he did not want to select a female employee because they tend to cry often.

Although I thought this question and the comment were absolutely inappropriate, I kept my mouth shut and answered all of the questions hoping for the position, and I got it. I remember everything went very well at first. I guess he was happy with my performance and language capability.

Our workplace required both Japanese and English ability, and I was his only employee who holds bachelor's degree from a U.S. school. He often took me to other offices and proudly introduced me to the people as his bilingual assistant. (I was not hired as his assistant!)

Shortly after, I started searching for promotion opportunities. I was not thrilled that I earned the least amount of money with the highest education in my office. When I turned in my application for a higher grade position, he advised me to stay and gave me an unofficial future promotion promise.

It was a mistake. I watched someone else hired for the position, trained and moved up. While I was still receiving same small paychecks, he kept feeding me new projects which weren't on my job description. I accomplished those projects and they brought great result.

We were able to fill the entire vacant engineer positions that have been constantly shorthanded. We even ended up with a big list of potential candidates. Yet, I received no promotion. He granted on the spot cash award to my co-workers who took the credit for the end-result of my projects.

I do not know what I have done or said to him for him to become a total jerk to me. He started ignoring my morning greetings. He only spoke to me when he absolutely needed; most of the communication was done through e-mails. What hurt me the most was that he often took all of my co-workers and some of MY friends who worked in the other office out for restaurants on lunch break and weekends.

I never received an invitation for this event. This forty-something man in a supervisory position kept playing total favoritisms against me (I was only twenty-four at that time.) I think my defense mechanism erased most of his hurtful comments and behavior. All I remember is how much I hated coming to work every morning knowing my boss would not talk to me.

My friends later told me that they felt very sorry for me to be treated that way. When I was selected for another position, he did not waste any time and released me in two days.

By that time, I had worked in the personnel office for a year and a half, and I had never seen anyone being released that soon. I didn't even have to train anyone. All he told me was to make sure I will leave instructions to the person who will fill my position.

As I mentioned before, I still have no clue what went wrong. I definitely started off as his favorite, and things turn 180 degrees. It is possible that I was his first female employee who was not afraid of speaking her opinion. Someone told me later that around that time, he was having a problem with his wife.

About ten years later, I attended one of my friend's wedding. My old boss and I happened to share a table at the reception. By the time, we had both became different people; he a mellower older man (reconciled with his wife, I heard), and me a thicker skinned married woman. In addition, being away from him for years made easy for me to share old time stories with him and at last, he apologized for his past behavior!

It was good to know that I did not do anything wrong to be treated that way. Yet, I still do not know the exact reason.

Asking this employee "do you cry?" is a signal that he seemed to have a personal problem dealing with women. As it turned out, at the time he hired this employee, he actually was having a difficult time with his domestic situation. Perhaps there was a lot of crying going on at home.

It looks as though the jerk-manager was transferring his lack of attention at home to this employee, until she made a point of speaking up for herself. That was when her manager realized he could not control her. As long as he felt that she was under his total control, she was his favorite.

The fact that he apologized for his behavior is an indication that he realized that he was suffering from a personal problem at the earlier time. Managers need to understand that personal problems cannot interfere with proper behavior on the job.

Staying in a miserable job has an effect on everything. It hurts you, your family, your co-workers and the company. One of the theories in Wake up! Wise up! Win! is if you are not having more fun than misery on a job, start to look for another job.

Episode # 6

The following is another tale about bosses lacking integrity and trustworthiness. I actually know of employees who have resorted to secretly tape-recording conversations with their bosses because of this type of problem.

Working under the direction of someone you do not trust is very stressful. You are constantly on guard for the time the unethical boss lies about you.

I've had my share of bad experiences with a previous manager. She was not my direct manager, but our department works closely with her department. In my previous position, I used to have more direct contact with her.

Even though this person was in management, she acted very unprofessional and sometimes. It got to the point where I would not go into her office to speak with her by myself, otherwise she would change everything I would say. So, I refused to meet with her alone, and I would take notes of everything she told me.

The worst thing is since she was in management, the other managers believed her when she made up lies about conversations we supposedly had, but that I never knew about that until later. If we did have a conversation, then she made up her own story. I'm glad she's gone, because I was already considering finding another job after working for this district for almost 15 years.

When someone tells lies about you, it attacks you self-esteem. You begin to wonder if your associates believe what the liar is saying. You start to feel distant from your peers, and you feel socially rejected.

One of a person's basic needs is social acceptance and positive self-esteem. Low self-esteem is probably the cause of most bigotry in the world.

A person who lies about someone else is suffering from his or her own low self-esteem. When he or she lies about others, it is an attempt to feel better than the others. Jerks want to feel like they are better than the persons they are lying about.

There is no place in the workplace for bigotry and discrimination. It creates tension and disharmony in an organization. Jerk-managers who bring their personal agendas to the office are not loyal to their workers, nor are they loyal to their company.

Episode #7

The next narrative provides a look at several obvious failures on the part of this employee's jerk-manager. As in most cases, this supervisor is lacking many of the positive traits of leadership that their employees desire.

The biggest jerk-manager I ever had was this guy named (....)
Now taking into consideration that I worked at a large packing house
with 200+ men and the only women were the 6 of us in the office. It did
not give this guy a free pass to humiliate anyone at any time.

Sometimes I think he would set people up for failure, just so he
could go out and scream and yell in front of their entire area of people.
He was an even bigger jerk because he chewed tobacco everywhere he
went and would spit it anywhere outside and into soda bottles at his
desk (INSERT BARFING NOISE HERE) He would never ask for
anything only bark orders and tell you what to do never explaining it.

I dodged him pretty well the first 3 years I was there, but in my
last week before being "let go" he came to me yelling, and got in my
face because I did what I was told by my supervisor and he didn't like
it. So, I told him to F** off and he could do my job the rest of the day. I
actually stayed the rest of the week and on Friday I had my last check.

I think we can go down the line and find that this jerk-manager registers a negative on each one of the 24 positive traits employees expect of their managers. He lacks personal integrity, is not trustworthy, has little or no ethics, is unreliable and he is surely not loyal to his company or his workers. He is certainly lacking in sociability, has poor communication skills, and falls short in all management skills as well.

Some jerk-managers think that because they work in physically demanding or rough working conditions they can be crude and rude. Regardless of the atmosphere in which you work, everyone deserves respect.

Episode # 8

Most astute managers are normally concerned with their employees' social and self-esteem needs. Occasionally, managers face situations bordering on an employee's survival and safety needs. This episode deals with this employee's physical survival and safety needs as well as her need to be accepted.

Unfortunately, in July of 2008, I was diagnosed with epilepsy. Since then, I have had about 10 epileptic episodes. I experienced a seizure on Saturday May 9, 2009.

The next day, I went to church. I attend the same church as the manager who was over my immediate supervisor at the time. I spoke with my supervisor's manager and let her know that I wouldn't be at work the following day (Monday). She understood my reason for not being able to go to work and said she would let my supervisor know what was going on with me.

The following day I didn't call in to speak with my supervisor because I was under the impression that she already knew the situation.

I went to work on the Tuesday after my epileptic episode, not knowing what was about to happen concerning the understanding about my situation.

"Why weren't you at work yesterday?" I told her my reason for not being there, and I also informed her of my conversation with her manager.

She then raised her voice and said, "She told me what was going on, BUT, you were still supposed to call me!" At that point, I was speechless because I couldn't believe someone could be so rude. Although I wasn't looking for any special attention, she should have been more polite.

Essentially, this jerk-manager was more concerned about her position of importance than her employee's personal welfare. People get sick. If you make an employee feel guilty, because he or she has to take off of work because they are sick, it makes them feel afraid to stay home when they really need to do so. Actually, in the restaurant trade, it is against the law to come to work ill.

Her boss even admitted that she knew why she was not at work. Instead of making the employee feel better by asking how she was feeling, she made her feel rejected and not worthy of personal concern.

Episode # 9

In my book, *Wake up! Wise up! Win!* I propose this theory: "If your fun factor is not considerably greater than your personal stress factor, sooner or later you are going to have a serious personal problem."

This next story is a good example of why I conjured up that theory.

Working for a jerk is one of the worst life experiences I have had. It makes going to work every day unbearable and affects every aspect of your normal life. I worked for a jerk for a total of three years in my four year tenure at (....). Allow me to share that experience with you.

My manager was dishonest, unethical and I question his morals too. He was dishonest because he would lie to customers and mislead them just to get them to sign agreements with the company.

The more customers we had the better our store looked. His would say. "better to fly under the radar". But then, when customers came into to discuss their services and the agreement, he would mysteriously come up missing, or he would pawn the customer off on some unsuspecting customer service representative.

He was unethical because he would show favoritism toward the pretty female employees, allowing them to call out sick for the day, take extended lunches and give the female employees sales they did not earn.

He was hoping this would boost his dating opportunities with one of them or several of them. His morals were screwed up too!

He was dating a sales associate when I started working there, but forgot to tell her he had wife in another state. He was dating this poor girl for a year before his estranged wife called the girl with the heart wrenching news.

Eventually, he was transferred due to a sexual harassment case brought against him by another female associate. Apparently, he grabbed her buttocks one night after work while the two of them we were closing the store.

Ultimately, he was fired due to theft! I learned a lot while working at this store, and I have plenty of gray hair to attribute to the stressful environment I was working within.

We actually had a few managers to come through our store after he was fired, and I think there may not have been one that displayed great ethical and moral values.

The jerk was veteran. I think that had something to do with it. People love to hire veterans under the assumption that they have great morals and discipline.

I hope that this is an extreme case and that not all jerk-managers are this bad. Obviously, this military veteran lacked all of the good things that this naïve employee assumed he possessed.

We can go down the list of the 24 positive traits employees want to see in a good leader and see that this jerk-manager fails miserably on each one. He has no personal values, little personal assets and no people skills. His management skills were totally inadequate.

It is very difficult for anyone with any principles to work in this type of hostile and dishonest environment. Working with someone this devious and this vulgar, places too much stress on honest people.

Although he did eventually get his comeuppance, he certainly did a lot of damage in the meantime. Undoubtedly, it seems that his behavior certainly left scars in the organization and on the employee submitting this story. Luckily, things got better for this writer after the jerk-manager was replaced and a new manager came on board.

Chapter Three

Personal Assets

The second area of personal traits we will study is personal assets. A person's personal assets provide him or her with the means for making proper decisions regarding the job at hand and the people he or she manages.

Personal Assets include being sufficiently educated, having creative vision and critical thinking ability. Effective managers should possess all of these necessary assets. Personal Assets determine our ability to evaluate situations, create possibilities, and make reasonable decisions.

Episode # 10

We start this chapter with a tale of enduring anger brought on by a jerk-manager. The storyteller chooses the word "despised" to indicate the great extent of the pain she experienced under this supervisor.

It is a short anecdote, nonetheless, with a powerful message. Managers need to know what they are doing. If they do not, chaos will inevitably result.

I had a manager that I absolutely despised, because she didn't know the first thing about what she was managing. This made it very difficult to go to her with questions - she wouldn't know the answer.

And she was not very personable either. I ended up taking her place, and since I know my department inside and out, I always have the answer. (And if I don't, I know how to find it.)

This story leads to my theory of the *Five Knows* in my book, *Wake up! Wise ! Win!* It deals with what managers need to know in order to make good decisions.

- *"Knowing what you know, when you know it."*
- *"Knowing what you don't know, when you don't know it."*
- *"Knowing what you need to know."*
- *"Knowing who knows what you need to know."*
- *"Knowing how to get them to let you know what they know."*

Having sufficient job knowledge does not mean that a manager must know everything. However, a manager must understand the limitations of his or her knowledge, and must understand that employee input is one of a leader's most valuable resources.

When the episode writer says, *"And if I don't, I know how to find it,"* she understands that the real job of a manager is to help his or her workers find the answer to their problems.

Managers who try to bluff their way through the day are easy to spot. They really lack self-confidence, and contrary to their know-it-all persona, they do not perform very well.

Episode # 11

Our next story deals with a very common situation found in many businesses, especially small businesses. The sad reality is that many times people get a promotion for the wrong reasons.

Often times, promotions just fill a void and upper management promotes the closest person available. Sometimes this works out. More times than not, it is a disaster waiting to happen.

For high level management and business owners, placing people in managerial positions is a very responsible job.

One of the things that I have come to see with some managers is that they only received their title because they were skilled at the job they did. Just because someone is good at a particular job does not make them a leader or a manager of people.

So many times, I think that the old school of thought was that people naturally wanted to progress forward because they did a good job.

Once I worked for a supervisor who didn't know the job. That wasn't the problem. Instead of trying to learn the job, he would ask me to make the decisions. However, when someone questioned the decision, he would blame me for it instead of standing behind me.

I stand behind whatever decision I make, but I couldn't defend myself because I was usually blamed during a managers meeting, which I wasn't invited to.

Instead of being an example, he would always try to get out of doing work. This in turn put more work on me because I was the Team Lead. He would go and sit down until the other managers came in the morning.

Then he would buy me a pop at the end of every shift as to say "does this make up for it". If he wanted to by my affection it was going to cost more than that. When we took our concerns to the Plant Manager, she said he was an engineer, so to her I guess that meant he was a great manager. That made it worst because we felt like he thought that having a "title" excused him from trying.

It wasn't just me or the shift that felt that way. There was a consensus among all the shifts. When we downsized he was one of the first to go.

This storyteller is describing a universal problem. It stems from promoting a person who might have good job skills, yet is lacking sufficient interest in, and or, preparation for supervising other. Some people do not want the responsibility of management, and in turn, do not handle the job well.

People generally fail at management for two main reasons: 1) they are not prepared to handle the responsibility, and or, 2) they do not want the responsibility,

Regardless of the reason, jerk-managers who are not equipped to handle the job will usually have problems supervising their employees. If a manager suffers from low self-esteem, the chances are they will not be able to discern how their own behavior impacts their employees' self-esteem.

Episode # 12

The account below tells of a case of classic burnout. Hard work seldom causes burnout. Yet hard-to-work-for bosses certainly do cause lots of burnout.

Dreading the idea of going to work in the morning is a sure signal that burnout is on its way. The saddest thing is when someone thinks he or she has no alternative but to stay in a job they hate.

When I first came in the state, I worked at a travel agency as a webmaster. I have worked with my supervisor who is very demanding and controlling.

I don't like a person who abuses their power; someone who is strong to weak people, and weak to powerful people. My supervisor had this kind of character, which I hate the most.

Also, I had no freedom. I had to report every hour wherever and whenever I go, whatever I do. I found myself working for a person who would be better off employed as a prison guard.

She was cruel for the sake of being cruel, took advantage of her position over others and lacked real people skills. She takes what she wants for herself, ignoring what other people say or want, ignoring how less powerful people react to her behavior, acting more rudely, and generally treating any situation or person as a means for satisfying her own needs.

From this lesson I've learned that leadership is important. Working with a jerk is one of the most persistent and harmful causes of job-related stress.

During this period, my days in the office felt eternal. I felt I was trapped in my job, suffered from less work and life satisfaction, had reduced commitment to my employer, along heightened depression, anxiety, and burnout.

We can see that the stress this employee feels is a direct result of her boss's total disregard for her employees' personal welfare. The boss is unpredictable, and I suspect totally irrational at times.

Her micro-management is a classic symptom of low self-esteem. She keeps track of her employees' every activity and controls their actions constantly. Some micro-managers are very capable supervisors and just want to make sure the workers will accomplish the job correctly. Other problematic managers do not feel qualified to do their own jobs and are usually fearful that their workers do not have the ability to do their jobs either. This is why they micro-manage.

Micro-managers tend to take away their workers' self-motivation and creativity. Very few people enjoy someone looking over their backs while they work.

Episode # 13

This next account deals with the need for managers to be reliable and responsible. Employees want to feel that their managers have the necessary confidence to lead them successfully.

Managers need to have good self-esteem and a high degree of self-confidence. Managers lacking these two important traits can be hazardous to a company's health.

The greatest thing that I have become to hate from managers I dislike are those managers without backbones. I see too often that managers don't have the ability to stand up and make decisions.

They are simply pushed over by employees and customers. That is not the way to handle the position of a manager and it gives others the power and ability to get away with whatever they want.

Businesses pay managers to make decisions. Managers who are unable or unwilling to make decisions are generally operating out of incompetence or fear of making a mistake. Whatever the reason, it is a serious problem.

In this case, this storyteller's manager is creating additional problems and headaches for the workers by not taking timely action to solve problems. This manager's problem is his lack of understanding that problems seldom go away by themselves.

Managers need to act promptly to assist their employees to handle business problems. Managers must serve their employees, not the other way around.

Episode # 14

"Don't confuse me with facts" could easily describe this manager's attitude. He is what we normally call a know-it-all.

Dictators are not leaders. They only have power because of the positions they hold. Leaders have power because people are willing to follow them. Perhaps, only in the heat of a battle, does the old idea of "just do it because I said so" work. That attitude does not work very well in today's volunteer military.

I have always had trouble dealing with the "I am the Boss, and what I say goes, and you just be quiet and do what I tell you." type of managers.

Usually these people are barely able to do the job that they have been assigned and are unwilling to hear anything that might confuse them, or put their knowledge of the job to any kind of a test. I very briefly worked in a dry cleaners a long time ago, and a new manager was hired who obviously knew nothing of the business.

He was constantly making mistakes that cost the company time and money. As opposed to fixing his own problems, he began to fault the workers. If I, or anyone else, were even a few minutes late, we would be admonished for contributing to the company problems.

He also assigned himself Quality Control King and would demand that a shirt that normally would pass inspection by the owner be completely repressed, which began to slow down production as well.

I dragged him in front of the owner one day and demanded he answer some very basic dry cleaning questions that anyone working in the field at all should know, and he was unable to respond to most of them with any sense of understanding.

I told the owner that I refused to work for this clown any longer and I quit. Two weeks later (after losing another good employee) the manager was fired. One of the worst types of manager is the one who BSs their way into the job and then just sits back and points fingers because they simply cannot manage. They are EVERYWHERE, like a plague.

Again, we see that lack of job knowledge can be a major cause of *jerkism*. The storyteller uses the term BS to describe this jerk's attempt to bluff his way through. Most people can spot a phony a mile away.

Not understanding the job and blaming others for his mistakes certainly falls under the area of lack of accountability. Managers who blame others for their own shortcomings often become defensive and abusive. They lack critical thinking ability and have little creative vision for making things better or more efficient and effective.

Chapter Four

Social Attitudes

People Skills fall next in the line of management expectations that employees have of their mangers. People Skills are broken down into: 1) Social Attitudes, 2) Communication Skills, and 3) Employee Support.

Social Attitudes include the following: Friendliness, Respectability, Impartiality, Fairness, and Respect for workers.

Episode # 15

In this case, this arrogant jerk has little people skills and displays ineffective management skills as well. Arrogance is the enemy of cooperation and congeniality.

Most people resent "smart asses." Most people do not like braggarts and know-it-alls. It is hard to deal with people who do not wish to learn anything new.

Arrogance does seem to be the common "jerk story" theme. I have been around a lot of arrogant managers and so-called leaders, and not surprisingly, they all seem to fade away in time.

I think their arrogance drives them out because they are unwilling to admit that they don't know everything, and therefore they are unwilling to hire good people to make up for what they don't know.

They instead seem to hire people that they make sure don't know more than they know, and therefore it makes them feel superior. This eventually causes them to make decisions that get them into trouble and eventually they are found on the outside looking in.

I agree that arrogance is a common theme in many of these *Jerk-Stories*. I also have personally witnessed the eventual downfall of many arrogant jerk-managers. Arrogance is not positive self-love. In reality, arrogance can easily be a way of hiding very low self-esteem.

In my observations, the lower the level of self-esteem and self-confidence, the greater the degree of arrogance. People with sufficient self-esteem and self-confidence do not fear others and they do not berate others. Nice people like other nice people.

All of these arrogant people would be wise to heed this old universal proverb.

Blessed Are The Gentle

Episode # 16

Inequality is the theme of this next *jerk-story*. This is about a person who does not understand that true leaders get their real authority only from those who wish to follow them.

Having a title and position does not make a leader. Leadership ability does. True leaders possess good personal assets and have great people skills. Leaders have high self-esteem and do not fear their employees.

In the military, there is fragile line between the Non-commissioned Officer (NCO) and Officer Corps-sometimes that line becomes blurry. The concept of the chain of command travels through both ranks and it somewhat intersects. Though every officer, even the lowest ranking officer, technically ranks higher than any NCO, even the highest ranking NCO, every individual takes on their role differently.

As a junior officer, it is somewhat challenging to enforce much of the authority given to me, when my counterparts have 20 or more years of service and experience than me. There is one person in particular, who has made my position exceedingly difficult.

On repeated occasions, I have heard military leaders say, "Inlisted must respect your rank and title, but you need to earn their respect as a person." I do not think this weathered person cares much about earning others' respect. I am sure there is some method to his madness, since he has progressed this far in his career, but I have not witnessed it yet.

I have had limited encounters with him in a one-on-one environment, but I like to keep it that way. At times that I see him, he has been overly condescending. The angry tone in his voice, the constant disgruntled expression on his face, and his unprofessional choice of words and intonation sends out an unfriendly, pompous, negative vibe to others.

I understand the idea that every person including young officers, should fear their standard bearer and regulation enforcer, but it seems that he has taken this role too far. He consistently demonstrates a disagreeable demeanor and indifferent attitude toward others that he works with. He does not exhibit supportive or understanding attitudes, which strong leaders oftentime possess. He makes it very clear that he is the subject matter expert and acts like he is the only one who could possibly make it as far as he has and has done it quite as good as he did. I am sure that his poor attitudes have developed over the years and maybe he is just in need of change, since he has been in the same location and position for several years.

The culmination of these characteristics make it difficult to work with an individual, especially if you must follow his orders or cooperate with him, and therefore, define 'jerk-like" behavior. In order to maintain a positive light on the situation,

I think of what my commander expressed to me recently, "Maybe it is better when you think someone is difficult to work with and they think that you are difficult to work with, than when you think very highly of someone, and they think you are an idiot."

Actually, it is always best to work for someone you think is smart and capable, and who thinks you are smart and capable too.

Early in my career, I learned that it was in my best interest to work for someone smarter and more capable than I am. You can learn from smart capable people, and they do not fear helping you with your career.

On the other side of the coin, managers who have little leadership ability often tend to fear their subordinates.

Episode # 17

This next story is the tale of a good manager gone bad. People can change and turn on you for many reasons. Perhaps we will never know why it happened in this case.

Managers who manage by emotion usually have problems separating their personal agenda from the business' agenda.

This paper is about a jerk manager I worked for when I first entered into the Information Technology field. My employment with this company started when the Director of Management Information Systems hired me.

Amazingly enough, this manager was fired within 1 year of starting with the company due to alcoholism. Once this manager's employment was terminated, I worked alone for approximately 6 months running the Information Technology department for this company. This included taking care of all the remote offices though out the south-central and southeastern part of the state, which often required driving several hours in my personal vehicle to arrive at the work location.

After, six months the company hired a person who came in as the Director of Management Information Systems. Upon arriving he told me, he intended to hire a new employee and have one person to be the network administrator, and the other being a field services technician.

This new manager offered me the Network Administrator job first, as he felt I deserved that position due to seniority. I accepted the position. He then hired another employee who also started doing network administration duties.

One day he called me in the office and asked about my work. At this time, he accused me of not getting the work done, and being gone for long periods without his knowledge. He knew it was due to the fact that I was still driving all over the state, putting high mileage on my personal vehicle and working very hard for this company.

I became very irate and realized he planned to get me fired and I knew it was time to resign. The interesting part was the company hired three people to replace me after I departed.

This could be a case of a manager not being willing to take the responsibility for the poor decisions he made. On the other hand, perhaps this manager deliberately set up this employee to fail. When a new manager takes over, a common method for getting rid of employees already in a job is to start a deliberate campaign to terminate them.

In either case, this appears to be a case of injustice. I would not want to continue to work for this manager under any circumstances. Would you?

Episode # 18

As in the previous tale, a common situation in many large organizations results from changing bosses. Particularly, when the old boss was great and the new boss is a jerk.

This can happen at any level within a company. It happens very often in companies with a high supervisor turnover rate.

My last job was in retail. When I first began the job, my department manager was amazing! She was so personable and was always on top of things. She even worked extra hours when we needed the extra help doing stock work.

Shortly after I got hired, she got promoted and we got a new department manager. She was the worst manager I had ever had.

Whenever I did something good or whenever I went above and beyond expectations, she said nothing. The second I did something wrong, she made sure to tell me about it. Not to mention, she wasn't friendly and was never around to help. But, when I did make a mistake, she made me feel like a complete idiot and was so mean about it.

What she should've done is explain where I went wrong and suggest ways to correct my mistakes or suggest ways to avoid it in the future. Managers can be positive even when things go wrong!

She lacks a caring attitude and makes no effort to acknowledge that everyone makes mistakes, including herself. The net result of this kind of behavior is employees who are reluctant to do anything on their own for fear of massive retaliation from the boss.

"I don't have time for you" could be an unspoken quote from this boss. Some jerk-managers think their time is too valuable to waste on helping their workers get their jobs completed efficiently and effectively.

This is certainly no way to help employees to become empowered to go on to bigger and better things. Employees need to be praised when the do good things and encouraged when they falter.

A good manager teaches his or her employees to improve. Managers should be servants, not tyrants.

Episode # 19

Is a good worker one who does a good job as quickly as they can and does it effectively? Or, is a good worker one who does mediocre work for many hours on end? The manager in this story thinks just being there is the more important thing.

At work there was a manager who was a problem. He believed in "face time" meaning that an employee's value was based on how much time they spent at work. This was obvious when it came to his hours, because he was constantly mentioning how he was the first one there in the morning. The worst part was that he would say "thanks for joining us today" sarcastically when other people came in at their scheduled start time.

When employees in his department would leave for the day, he would say "thanks for putting in a half day" or "glad you could be troubled to be here." Even after numerous complaints from employees and reprimands from human resources, nothing additional was done to correct his behavior.

I hear from former co-workers that he continues these actions today. He exhibits passive aggressive behavior that likely stems from his feelings of insufficiency. However, he didn't stop and is not being made to stop.

This manager's aggression has a negative effect on the office staff and reduces the employees' confidence in the ability of the human resources department to correct a damaging situation. Until this manager realizes the hurtful impact he has on others, the situation will continue.

Do you think that most people would react positively to this type of sarcasm? Teasing can be fun in the right atmosphere, but sarcasm is not joking around. It is hurtful and does not engender respect.

People should have fun at work. They should not be subject to ridicule and innuendo. Attacks on an employee's self-esteem are very destructive to self-confidence and self-motivation. In the case of widespread sarcasm, such as in this story, poor overall morale usually exists.

Episode # 20

Once again, in the next chronicle, arrogance rears its ugly head. This jerk thinks life is all about her. She is not concerned about anyone else.

Evidently, as a child she was never taught the value of please and thank you. "Please" and "Thank you" are a manager's greatest people skills assets.

I had a manager who was a jerk, mainly because she was her entire universe. She is the type of person who doesn't care who she knocks down on her way up, as long as she gets there. She has a nasty personality (unless you can help her get to the top). She makes demands and doesn't ask nicely. I'm glad to not work for her anymore!!

Obviously, this jerk has no loyalty to her workers. She lacks integrity and is unethical. People with this obvious lack of social graces have a tough time with lasting relationships.

Unfortunately, many organizations are full of these bullies. They have little regard for anyone else and step on anyone on their way to the top. Characteristically, because they do not develop a support structure, they usually fail when they get there, if they ever do.

Episode # 21

There is a huge turnover in the restaurant business, especially in fast-food operations. Easy entry with little skills into the fast-food industry creates this high turnover rate.

The effects of poor management added to a lack of employee skills, creates a recipe for much unrest in fast-food outlets. The story below helps to explain why this is so.

In the restaurant business, I feel that most of the managers I have worked with have been really big jerk-managers. The worst one was a manager who drank all night, and who would proceed to hit on me all the time and embarrass me in front of guests making comments about my personal life.

My husband, my boyfriend at the time, finally got involved because one night he said something about my cleavage in front of him and this was the last straw.

I had talked to my big boss numerous times about his inappropriate behavior, but unfortunately, they were good friends and were drinking together most of the time. I finally had to resign because I could not take the sexual harassment any longer.

Looking back, I really wished that I would have filed a suit against him because I feel that he needed to be stopped from doing this to any other women who worked for him. I recently heard that the restaurant actually went under and was closed, so this was pretty good news for me.

Sexual harassment in particular and employee harassment in general is a common complaint against jerk-managers. It stems from a total lack of personal respect for the employees by their managers. Harassment works in both ways, male or female.

Employees subject to constant harassment of any kind find it difficult to enjoy their workplace. As did this storyteller, when it gets bad enough, they quit,.

While this kind of jerkism on the job is illegal, employees seldom file complaints for fear of retaliation. Experience shows that top management seldom, if ever, admits that an employee has been harassed. Instead, they accuse the employee of insubordination.

In many ways, a person lacking sufficient self-esteem does not consider that anyone else deserves any greater degree of respect than he does or she does.

Harassment on the job is just another case of bullying. It is probably a carryover from childhood. Can this type of bully change? Sadly, that is doubtful.

Episode # 22

Here is another tale of woe from the restaurant trade. This industry is full of young workers working for poorly trained and inadequate supervisors.

Is there any question about why there is such a great turnover rate in the fast-food industry?

When I first started working, I worked at a fast food franchise and had the most jerkish manager in the world (or so it felt like).

Being that there are many young employees in the fast food industry, we (especially me in this incident) I was looked down upon. I was literally belittled and screamed at.

I remember the day my friend quit/got fired, the manager who knew we were friends pulled me aside the next day to tell me she knows that I saw my friend leave and then she had the nerve to say, "I just wanted to bring you aside to say if you want you can leave too!" I had nothing to do with what had happened with my friend that day, it was a personal issue that occurred.

Then the day I put in a week notice to leave, because I was going to go to college, she pulled me aside again to tell me that if I wanted I could leave sooner because I would never make it. She stated college is too hard and I am not smart enough, and if she was still in fast food business then I'm definitely not going to make it either.

Well the last time I checked she is still there, I am banned from working at any of these companies again because she put a bad rep out on me. But, it doesn't matter because to prove her wrong, I will be graduating with my Bachelor's degree next year. Goes to show that she was wrong!

This is a clear example of a supervisor with such low self-esteem that she has to put down others to make herself feel better. It seems that since she thinks that going to college is too hard for her, then it must be too hard for her employees.

This transference of negative thinking is routine among many jerk-managers who feel little hope of improving their own station in life. Generally, people who have never been encouraged to do something themselves, do not know how to encourage others.

Sadly, this behavior often comes about because the person did not receive much, if any, positive reinforcement as a child. Good managers always provide support and encouragement for their employees.

Episode # 23

Have you ever wondered why some managers hire or promote someone and then do everything they can to sabotage that person's career? I have witnessed this many times.

This next detailed account illustrates this painful phenomenon.

I had a manager in sales a few years who promoted me to be his assistant manager. This guy would tear me down in front of other employees when he was not happy with me, then when I did some that made him happy, like make a sale, he would sing my praises in front of other employees.

This man would make comments that were unethical in the workplace. He would also call me and tell me that I was needed in the morning meetings when I was sick. During a time that I stayed sick for two weeks, I went to all the meetings and then went back home to bed. This guy was a complete jerk and I quit because I had words with him on several occasions and I just got tired of working with him. Even after numerous complaints from employees and reprimands from human resources, nothing additional was done to correct his behavior.

I hear from former co-workers that he continues these actions today. He exhibits passive aggressive behavior that likely stems from his feelings of insufficiency. However, he didn't stop and is not being made to stop.

This has a negative effect on the office staff and reduces the confidence in the ability of human resources to correct a damaging situation. Until this manager realizes the hurtful impact he has on others and wants to change, the situation will continue.

Poor job knowledge and poor decision-making ability leads to poor management skills. Personal conflict on the job is one of the biggest factors relating to burnout from working with a jerk-manager.

Employees can only take personal attacks for so long before they retreat from the hostility. As this story shows, it does no good to fight this type of manager. In the end, flight is usually the best course of action.

Episode # 24

We end this chapter with two stories of personality conflicts at work   Managers who openly display a personal dislike for an employee make it very difficult for that employee to work in such a hostile environment. This narrative tells of such a case.

The Jerk boss I had was a guy hired as chief engineer by the company that bought out the company I was working for. I was in the position as acting Chief for over a year when he started.

He didn't like me from the start. He had very bad troubleshooting skills. So, every time that I was able to fix something that he couldn't he would get very upset. He actually started harassing me. Following behind everything I did and trying to find anything he could to write me up. Twice he resorted to yelling at me like I was his child.

This was unacceptable and I was very close to punching him in the face, but if I were to do that I would have been fired and he would have won. I instead told him that he was harassing me and I was going to HR to file a report. All harassment stopped immediately and we got along in a civilized manner from that point on.

As we see above, this story illustrates a problem that arose when a vindictive manager did not have sufficient job related education, had little critical thinking ability, and no creative vision. Of course, this jerk-manager also lacks almost every one of the other good managerial traits employees expect.

He could easily fit into the Jerk-Stories listed under all of the people skills and management skills. Luckily, he changed his behavior when confronted by the employee. More than likely, he continued his harassment of those employees who did not challenge him.

Episode # 25

The final story in this chapter is long and detailed. However, it perfectly describes the situation resulting because of jealousy toward her employee. This manager shows she is woefully unprepared for the role of leadership.

There is no place in management for such erratic and emotional behavior. Good supervision results from objective decisions made for the good of the company.

When I was in the military, I worked for a female NCO. She was the head of the support operations section within the unit. We were responsible for ensuring that we were fully capable of supporting upcoming missions and takings.

Everything was going well. She introduced me to the team and the team was running like a well oiled machine. We even had plans to make the team better. We were going to implement new and innovative ways to motivate the section to accomplish task done without being told. We had a system down to a science.

However, everything changed when she found out I was going to be promoted to NCO. As soon as she found out I was going to be promoted, she congratulated me.

However, then she found out that I had only been in for 12 years. She was surprised. Her demeanor changed. Then she stated that I was fast-tracking, but I ignored the comment. I did not pay it any attention until she stopped talking to me, and everything she had to say was through emails, unless we were in a meeting.

I could not understand it, because I sat less than five feet from her. However, she would walk to another office in order to speak with the rest of the supervisors. She started assigning me tasks that were related to the job; however, they were someone else's responsibility.

Nevertheless, I accomplished the tasks. On one occasion, she told me to write two standard operating procedures (SOPs). The first was on how to request items without using the standard supply system, and the second was a tactical standard operating procedure (TACSOP). A TACSOP is a brakedown on how each element (ie...medical, fuel, food, ammunition, water, and supplies) within our command will provide support to other units.

The SOP for the request of items was completed and placed on her desk in two weeks. The TACSOP was not going to be as easy. It would require a subject matter expert from each area to write up their capabilities and how they can provide support.

Even though I know what each section has, I can't write how they plan to use their resources. They will have to do that for themselves. I informed her on the matter, but she told me to make it happen. When I asked for guidance she gave none. She even had me wait all day for a meeting that never took place.

So, I started asking around. When I asked each section for their help they asked me why I was doing a TACSOP and I told them that I was instructed to write it by my supervisor. They all told me that that was not my job; it was the job of the supervisor to ensure I had all the write ups. Come to find out she had never done one.

Also, after three months of her telling me to do things she was supposed to be doing, I got tired and spoke to the commander. Before I could even complete my first sentence, he informed me that he already knew about the situation.

A few months later, a call came from the supervisor who serves as the advisor to her boss and I was moved a few days later to a better job. When she was informed that I would be moving she was not very happy. When I went back to visit, the SOP that I had written on the *request procedure was still sitting in her inbox the same place I had placed it five months prior.*

Jealousy is a destructive disease. In the workplace, it hurts both people. The jealous person suffers great internal stress and negative feelings toward the other person. At the same time, the person who is the object of the jealousy bears the brunt of the hostility shown them.

In this case, this jealous manager constantly harassed the storyteller. She gave her unfair extra workloads. She does not recognize her good work, and ostracizes her. This jerk-manager made her work life miserable.

Happily, her transfer solved her problem. Yet, it did not solve the problem for the other workers still working for this jerk-manager.

Chapter Five

Communication Skills

Communication Skills include, Effective Communication Skills, Acknowledges Good Work, and Available to Workers.

Poor communication is perhaps the number one problem with underperforming businesses and jerk-managers. Jerk-managers who cannot adequately explain the company's mission and goals do not have the necessary assets for achieving high performance.

Episode # 26

Nobody likes a know-it-all. This type of jerk-manager will generally fit the description of someone who would say, "don't confuse me with facts, my mind's made up." They do not want to hear any other ideas and think that they have all the answers.

In reality, when someone has all of the answers, they are very closed-minded and have only one vision, their own.

Arrogance and an unwillingness to listen to others are the common traits that I have noticed in "jerk" managers. Like someone said about managers getting set in their way, which to a point I understand.

Sometimes things have to be done in a certain way, which is not always the easiest or quickest way, but the reasons can be explained to subordinates. I also know firsthand how irritating it can be to have employees come up telling you that things should be done this way and not that.

Some people think that know it all, even if they have only been introduced to the idea they are claiming to be a expert on. But, taking the time to listen and communicate what's what is not asking too much.

I know that I was always willing to hear people out and sometimes they have really good ideas that save a lot of time and effort.

Communication is a two-way street. It takes both senders and receivers. Many jerk-managers such as described in the first part of this story do not understand walking on the receiving side of the street. On the other side of the street, the storyteller gives us an idea of what a good listener offers to the company's success.

Poor communication is the downfall of many organizations. Managers who do not realize that every employee has something to contribute are missing out on valuable information.

Episode # 27

Arrogance and ignorance usually go together in creating jerk-managers. Anyone who thinks they know everything is certainly arrogant. No one knows everything.

One thing that people who claim to know it all do not know is how to manage people. "My way or the highway" is not going to win many followers.

Some managers have a sense of "I know what works or I know what's best because I'm the manager." That is not true at all. In management, you have to be willing to listen to your employees and sometimes activate what they are saying.

The majority of the employees have a better insight into what works, because they are involved with the services you are offering daily. So, for a manager you must be open to ideas and suggestions that work for the best of that company.

When I worked at this hospital, I worked for a terrific manager, she was always open to suggestions as to how to make the department run smoothly. Not only was she open, she ran pilot trials on a lot of those suggestion from us employees, because she knew we were dealing with the doctors and patients on a daily basis and we encounter many problems that needed to be addressed and adjusted in order to provide outstanding patient care and customer service.

I loved her management skills because not only did she teach she was willing to learn.

In the past, although not mentioned in detail, this storyteller has obviously worked for a manager who did not care what his or her workers thought. The storyteller goes on to give an example of a supervisor who did listen. As a result, the hospital did not reap the rewards of every employee's thinking.

The storyteller's last sentence gives the key to success. Businesses must be learning organizations. Being willing to learn is the only way to keep up with the ever-changing world of business.

Episode # 28

Mean talk and insults do not make for happy workers. Especially in an office environment, talk should be professional and polite at all time. Employees should not be subject to degrading comments and deliberate put-downs. You do not have to be friends with the people you work with, but you should be friendly.

This story tells a tale of someone who does not understand the value of "please and thank you." Most successful leaders learn to be polite as infants.

Before I became a manager, I had a senior manager that thought it was his right to make remarks about another subordinate's age. That person wasn't one of those whiny, stop teasing me types of people. He usually laughed it off and went about his day.

I noticed the person's job effort and team interaction starting to melt, and at lunch one day asked him about it to make sure everything was alright. He told me about these instances, admitted to me the age comments were wearing on his nerves as team members are now adding to the stress of the manager's comments on being old at 46 and the rude jokes and implications never stopped.

I addressed this with the team, but instead of going back to the way things had been before this manager started, the team ostracized the member who was being insulted. He finally got so frustrated with the comments and innuendos that he quit out of stress over the matter.

Burnout is a customary result of an employee feeling that management is persecuting him or her. People can only stand personal attacks for so long before they call it quits.

It is extremely difficult to maintain a high level of self-esteem when you are constantly the object of insults and innuendo.

Episode # 29

Every employee has a right to respect. Many good employees are lost because of a manager's lack of respect for the dignity of their employees.

The Bill of Rights holds true at the office as well as everywhere else. Many jerk-managers do not understand the meaning of "common courtesy."

I had a jerk-manager who was also a micro-manager. We work on commission, so we have monthly goals. These goals are set by our market managers and are market wide.

My manager would take it upon himself to hike the goals up and make us reach higher ones. We would also get written up for not meeting these goals. In his mind, it was never an issue because he called it his "coaching tactic."

He would also write you up if you weren't 15minutes earlier than your shift, marking it as a lateness.

His Philosophy was if you are not early, you are late. It was not pleasant at all to work for him because you were constantly being reprimanded and there was very little recognition.

As a manger you have to be able to recognize opportunities as well as strengths and make sure that you are able to speak on both of them. As an employee, I would like to be recognized when I am doing something right; it creates a better relationship between boss and employee. That way when you have to tell an employee they are doing something wrong, it is better received.

This jerk-manager certainly falls short on personal integrity, ethics, loyalty and reliability. We can also see that this jerk had poor people skills, and scores a big negative grade on management skills as well.

Managers who behave in this fashion kill the self-motivation that most employees have. This type of manager has no realization of what a pat on the back can do to the employee's self-esteem. Would you want to work for someone like this?

Episode # 30

The next narrator has evidently experienced working in a very negative atmosphere involving a female manager. It seems that many female employees feel extra pressure working under a female supervisor.

Conceivably, this gender pressure could be only in the minds of the employees, while in truth, their female managers are not being at all unfair to their female underlings. Although, in this case, it appears that the type of female supervisor in this story is, in fact, a jerk-manager.

I speak for myself when I have worked for managers of the same sex (woman). I find that they can be jealous or defensive. Jerk-like behaviors are more frequent as woman are very catty!

I again feel like there is more competitiveness and envy amongst an all female staff. Nonsense issues are more frequent. Gossiping and knit-picking even among so-called managers are frequent too. I have witnessed this trend. Am I alone?

Actually, this same story comes up many times. It seems to be more common in situations where a female manager is struggling to compete for promotions in a "good-old-boy" organization. I need not point out that competition for advancement does not excuse this bad behavior.

Perhaps, asking workers to work harder in order to be better than their male counterparts is not bad in itself. Nevertheless, when accompanied by degradation, gossip and defensiveness, it becomes very destructive to office morale.

Episode # 31

The following tale paints a picture of the opposite situation concerning gender differences. Overbearing behavior of a male boss against his female employees is also a serious organizational problem.

No matter which gender is at fault, gender bias is not good for organizational health. Gender bias is as destructive as race bias, ethnic bias, or any other bias.

When I worked at my previous job, this boss was very unfair to women as far a being a good leader and taking responsibility of the department. He thought all women should be at home taking care of children and keeping house because his wife at home.

I have worked in several different departments such as Records, Finance and my last job change was in security where I was a supervisor over the department. When something would go wrong in the department, he would always blame me and not the other supervisor, because he was a man.

When we had a meeting with all the staffs in the department, he would give men most of duties in the department. If you would ask him a question, his answer would be, we will talk about it a later date.

He never wanted to hear any new ideas that would make the department have less problems. He would also say that I am the manager and the department has to be in good order especially for inspection.

The other people in the department would talk about him to each other, but would never say nothing to him because they would fear losing their jobs. He didn't get along well with all of the staff and would blame you for all the things that went wrong.

He never gave any inspiration or encouragement and would disapprove of you trying to better yourself if you decided to return to school to further your education. He was a boss who was always unhappy and had a bad communication problem when it came to his staff's work details and assignments.

Not only was this jerk-manager a bigot, he was also a poor communicator, had an obnoxious personality, and had no people skills whatsoever. Although he thinks he is displaying a positive and responsible commanding presence, he surely suffers from low self-esteem and little self-confidence.

He gets no respect from his employees. In reality, he had little self-esteem and little self-confidence. Self-confident people do not put others down.

Episode # 32

It is quite evident from the tone of this account that it is from an employee who is still upset about the jerk described in this story. Some bad job experiences can certainly have long-lasting consequences.

The storyteller held out for as long as she could. In the end, she succumbed to burnout.

I worked for her for two (2) years. She hired me out of college as a paralegal in her law firm. On the surface, she seemed like a sweet woman who has it all.

However, that is not so. She was an anal SOB. She loved to micro-manage me. She would scream and holler when things were not going her way. She would scream about my desk, her desk, and the office. She loved to make you feel beneath her. She would bring her problems from home into work.

At times, she would tell me of the problems. When she brought outside problems into the workplace, she would analyze my work even harder. She even cursed me out. I put a quick stop to that. I told her that I was quitting, and a few other things that should not be mentioned. A year later, I quit working for her.

Working for someone who screams, and rants and raves is certainly no fun. It is amazing that this storyteller remained in the job for another year.

This is another case of the manager being unable to separate her personal life from her business life. Good managers behave in a professional mode of behavior. Good managers base business decisions on good business practices, not on emotions.

Within the limitations of the business, managers should be compassionate and understanding of their employees' personal needs. Obviously, this jerk does not care about her employee's feelings. As managers, we need to understand the concept that your people will make you or break you.

Episode # 33

Dishonesty is one of the main complaints against jerk-managers. When we look at good communication skills, honesty is a fundamental requirement.

This account paints a picture of backbiting, duplicity, and taking credit for someone else's good work. It is not a pretty picture. Unfortunately, it is common.

I worked for a jerk in the military. I believe there were a multitude of reasons why this person was a jerk. One reason in particular, I think, the biggest kind of jerk there can be is being two-faced.

When I first began to work for this person, she seemed very nice. She was always willing to listen to problems, to help when and where she could, and to set the right example of what a leader should be.

When I arrived, I was the most senior rank of her subordinates, so naturally some issues arose. She was there to help sort out the problems, or at least give us (her subordinates) the direction we needed to come up with our own solution.

Things went on this way for a few months - a problem arose, she helped fix it - until an instance came up where she was not there to help. Being the senior person remaining, it was my job to perform conflict resolution. So, I sat down with one of the other workers and we discussed the issue.

During that conversation, both of us realized that we were not the cause of most of the problems in the unit. We discovered that the supervisor was actually the cause of a lot of the problems. She would do or say something to one of us that would ultimately lead to conflict with the other. Then she would step in and provide the solution.

She was either trying to feel better about herself by helping "solve" conflict, or show her superiors that she was a competent leader because she could solve these problems. And conflict resolution was not the only scenario that she claimed responsibility for.

When one of us would excel at something or reach a distinguished achievement, she would take the credit for developing us to attain that achievement. Most often she actually had nothing to do with our achievement. We most often did things on our own or helped each other.

A good leader, I think, who is given praise for developing their subordinates, would defer that praise to the hard work their subordinates put in, not take credit for the work they may or may not have done. We, the subordinates, learned our situation quickly enough that it did not have an effect on our working relationship or our ability to accomplish our mission.

Fortunately that jerk was not in the position very long before she left the military. Last I heard, she was a private masseuse.

She has no subordinates, which is probably a good thing because now she cannot take credit for the accomplishments of others and she cannot create conflict just to be the resolution.

This storyline backs up my theory that most jerk-managers eventually get their comeuppance. In the meantime, their employees suffer.

Although the workers were able to work around this jerk's poor management skills, this basic question remains unanswered. How much more productive could they be with a good leader?

Episode # 34

Tyranny exists in many workplaces. It usually comes in the form of a jerk-manager as described in this next case. This office situation is equal to a dictatorship.

Again, "My way or the highway" is a good slogan for this manager's conduct. Threats are not a positive way to achieve positive relationships and teamwork.

I have said before that I have been in some form of leadership role since I was sixteen. As I have changed companies over the years, I often had to work my way up to a leadership role. Personally, the best learning experience for me was also the worst experience.

I had a manager who constantly threatened to fire people almost daily; this person was never happy about anything. He would talk down to people and yell at them if they did not catch on as quickly as he thought.

As an employee, I got the gossip firsthand about how people really felt about this person; although people respected the title, they did not respect the person. The thing that I learned from this person has been the most valuable lesson of all.

People will do exactly what you ask if they only respect the position. However, if they respect the person, they will generally go beyond what you ask because they want to. People work for people not companies.

This jerk has little hope of developing effective communication skills. He seems to operate from a perpetual feeling of unhappiness. Negativity breeds negativity. No one wants to work in such an unpleasant atmosphere.

Generally, people only stay in such situations because they have little opportunity to go elsewhere. The result is a mediocre organization, with mediocre management, and mediocre performance.

When it comes to gaining respect from his workers, this jerk-manager reaps no rewards. How can anyone expect to have happy employees under this circumstance? No doubt, this lucky storyteller was able to move on to bigger and better things.

Episode # 35

Partiality rears its ugly head in this episode. It fits the common idea of "it's who you know, not what you know." Nepotism is the downfall of many organizations.

Organizations are only as strong as their weakest link. Placing someone in a position of power simply because he or she is a relative does not create a strong chain of management.

I did once have a manager who was very arrogant. I believe what helped him be so arrogant was his father-in-law was a VP in the organization. He really had a way of talking to people in a way that was very low, as though he was better than anyone else. Most often people may respect the title, but not the person.

We must admit not all sons, daughters, in-laws and other relatives of business owners fall into the jerk category. Indeed, many great business owners are second and third generation family members. However, sometimes people who think they are immune to termination feel they can behave as badly as they wish.

When senior managers protect their jerk relatives, the problem gets serious. Incompetent second and third generation family members cause many companies to go bankrupt.

In reality, jerk-managers who give favored status to any employee, relative or not, cause problems within their organizations. Experience shows that favoritism breeds contempt from the other employees, and has a negative effect on teamwork.

Chapter Six

Employee Support

Employee support includes showing an interest in and providing personal support for workers. Workers who feel that their managers do not treat them as human beings suffer from a lack of belonging.

Jerk-managers are often the reason why their employees' needs for social acceptance are unmet. Employees who feel rejected have a difficult time with their self-esteem.

Episode # 36

I worked for a manager who felt that a good manager was one that was disliked by his employees. This manager would do everything in his power to promote disunity.

I worked as a banquet setup person at a hotel. Good production depended on everyone working together. If this manager saw others helping those who were not as fast as others, he would try to discipline both employees. It got to a point where employees would call in to be off for sick days when he was on location.

His analogy was to weed out the weak ones to make the team stronger, but we all felt strength was in numbers. Those who were slow would learn how to become faster when setting-up from others.

This manager treats his employees as if they were a team of draft horses or sled dogs. If you cannot keep up with the pack, then you do not belong on the team. This attitude leaves no room for variation in the levels of performance of the individual employees.

My theory on teamwork states that all team members need to help each other. In essence, those team members who do not help their other team members are the real problem. In football, for example: The best running back in the world would not make much yardage without good blockers clearing the way.

Episode # 37

Good managers care about us, help us and support us. They tend to spoil us. Unfortunately, as in this anecdote, it is even more frustrating to the employees when a jerk takes over from a previous good leader/manager in an organization.

Changes in department managers are routine in most larger companies. All too often, a new manager comes in thinking they have to make changes to establish their authority. Change for the sake of change is usually a disaster.

I used to work at a local insurance company in the state. When I first began in January 1999, my boss was super. She was great at teaching you new things and was always there to listen to you and help you out.

Things changed quickly when my boss decided to relocate with the company, and moved out of state. That is when the new boss took over, and she was a devil. She was not the approachable type. She was always too busy for you and acted like it bothered her to answer a question. She quickly took a disliking to me, because I was very good friends with the Vice president of our department.

I guess she felt threatened by my close relationship with him and his family. I was always the one getting extra work dumped on me. When I completed something and the management team liked it, she took all the credit. However, if I completed something that was not up to management's standards, I was the one held accountable.

My best friend also worked there. She went to lunch from 12:30-1:30. My lunch hour was from 12:00-1:00. I asked to change my lunch hour to match my friend's so we could start walking on our lunch hour. I was told no, because we didn't need to be fraternizing at work.

We could be friends, but it had to be away from work. My job duties consisted of the same tasks for 3 years straight before I quit. And even though it was the same monotonous job duties, I still had to have her approval on everything I completed. She would not let me just do my work.

When I decided to leave, I gave them a 3 week notice. The lady that was taking over my job duties was very intimidated by a computer. I decided to sit down and write down step-by-step instructions for each job task that I was responsible for, so that whoever was taking over would have a reference to look at in case they forgot how to do the task.

She took the reference sheets and shredded them. She told the lady that she did not need those reference sheets and that she was going to train her the proper way. She would always tell me that she was in charge of my pay raises. Prior to my resignation, my big boss never complained about the way I was doing things.

I am now working at the hospital. I am the Director of Human Resources and responsible for salary surveys and maintaining the pay scales for our employees. My old boss is now working at the same hospital as well. However, the difference is I am now upper management and she is not.

Karma is a bitch when the roles are reversed. She now acts like we were the best of friends at our old job. I guess that is because now I am in charge of her pay raises!

Well it appears that in this chronicle, the old saying, "be careful who you step on climbing your way up the ladder," is a good piece of advice.

When this supervisor was in charge, she exhibited a severe lack of self-confidence and she expressed it in several ways. She was jealous and vindictive. She feared that her employees would cause her problems if they were friends with each other at work.

She feared losing control, and took every opportunity to exert her authority over her employees, regardless of the consequences of her behavior. In the end, she lost total control over the storyteller.

Episode # 38

The next jerk-story tells a different story. Yet it is just as troublesome. Highly self-confident people tend to think they can work for any boss, even so-called tough ones. In spite of this, some people are so difficult to relate to it is best to avoid them if possible.

Too bad the term *tough* does not have universal meaning. Sometimes, as in this story, the term *tough* is a substitute for *tyrannical*.

I was a temp for an agency that I was referred to by a friend of mine. His friend was starting an employment agency and always had great opportunities. She would call me from time to time to see if I was happy at my current place of employment or when she knew of a job that offered more money.

I have been working for a very long time and have a ton of accounting, billing, and office experience. One day she called and told me about a great opportunity, but said the boss was difficult to work for and did I want to try it out.

Thinking that I have a good personality, experience, and I am a good worker with no bad track record, I'd be able to handle this lady with no problems. The money was excellent, the most I had ever made and the hours and location were both great.

I began to work for this lady and from day one she was always frustrated and crabby. I thought well maybe she doesn't feel like going through the training process again and since I wasn't familiar with her software program, she would have to have a little more patience.

The work load was so over whelming and being in a small office with just the two of us made my weeks harder and harder. She insulted me by making statements like "how could I say that I have Accounting experience and not know that software program." I had stated during the interview that I did not know the program and there was so much tension that I couldn't get up to go to the bathroom.

I dreaded going there every morning and since my boyfriend worked in the same building, we would commute together. One day after work, I cried the whole way home and never went back. I already felt bad about myself for not going to college, and then I couldn't catch on to the program because she was so scary that I couldn't concentrate, and to top it off with her comments, it was easy to see why nobody was lasting in this position.

A funny ending, one day she showed up to the office with a black eye that one of her friend's had given her, and that was the best day ever!

Every time someone mentions bad managers, she is the one and only that comes to mind. Later I became concerned that I had burned my bridge with my friend (the head hunter), but she called me a few months later to offer me a different job and told me that she figured if I did not make it at the first job, she wouldn't send another victim for that position.

On a positive note, my current boss is great with communicating and training.

I think this jerk-story again illustrates a theory from my book, Wake up! Wise up! Win! If you hate going to work in the morning, start looking for another job. Work should be fun, not misery.

Any boss who makes you cry, because of the way he or she treats you at work, is definitely a jerk of the worst kind. Working for someone who never has a kind word and never gives you an affirmation of your good work is a sure road to burnout.

Everyone needs to feel appreciated. In fact, experience shows that acknowledgment for good work is very important to most employees.

Episode # 39

This rather long story details so many jerkish behaviors it is hard to know where to begin analyzing this autocratic military manager.

This supervisor alienates people and makes everyone feel unappreciated and unacceptable. Working under these conditions is extremely stressful.

While stationed on board a ship one of my supervisors was a genuine JERK.

It didn't take me long to learn that he was in charge simply because he was the only med-tech on board. The man was a genius and could answer any and all questions when it came to medical. He was studying to become a Physician Assistant.

The problem I saw was even the patients he was seeing could not stand him, and many refused to be treated by him. When he had sick-call, patients would stay away and just preferred to suffer for the day. He had no people skills.

The really bad part about that is their supervisors understood and did not make them go to sick-call but sent them to their racks. One of us (other corpsman on board) would eventually get a call asking us to see their people. Of course, we understood and we took care of them.

He had a, "I wanna be liked personality" but we could not stand to even talk to him. His leadership style consisted of standing behind me, literally looking over my shoulder. When he wanted to discuss something with me he would stand to the side of me, behind me or in front of me and just stare at me. I had to say, "can I help you?" He then just grinned and said "yes, I need to speak with you about something when you finish."

Now you would think he would walk away and I would find him after I finished what I was doing. Oh no, he continued to stand there and stare at me. I was usually with a patient, so unless it was urgent I did not see a need to walk away and discuss anything with him until I finished with my patient.

He was the type of leader that stood for, do as I say because I told you to. He would actually say, "I gave you an order and I need you to do it now." I would try and explain maybe that I couldn't get to another step until I finished this one. His face would turn red with embarrassment and still demand what he wanted now.

He also has no organizational skills. When the department would get really busy, he would go into panic mode and just start throwing out orders for people. Sending staff to do things that just were not logical, and stop people when they were in the middle of a task.

When the supervisor came through, because things were in chaos, we did not hesitate to let him know. We tried to tell him but he would not listen to us. "Sir, I am following his orders."

I remember once when the supervisor came up front and yell what the H** is going on, I yelled back fast, "Yes sir, once again we are just following orders, but with your permission I promise you I can fix it. He looked at me and then at him and said," NOW, FIX IT NOW!".

Of course, the jerk did not like that and actually tried to counsel me after sick-call for disrespect. I simply put staff where they worked the best, assisted patients in the passage way that could either come back or need to be in one of our racks till we could get to them.. I got on the phone and called other staff that he had sent out of the department. That was stupid.

He sent them away because we were not busy yet but, of course, sick-call had just started and he didn't check the department. The others were young and quickly ran out of the department because they too knew it was going to get busy. Well, I yanked them right back. I told them in the future you go nowhere till after sick-call.

Next, because he was so slow at sick-call and he couldn't check a patient in correctly to save his own life, I asked the supervisor to please take him and let him assist you with patients. He understood and agreed. He too knew that with him out of the equation, staff and patients were more under control.

We could all see his lack of self esteem. I truly hated working for him, but I felt really sorry for him also. He knew he was not liked and it was not because he was our supervisor.

He had not a clue how to run a department or how to talk to his staff. He could not gain their trust and or respect, nor did he know how to. He had no idea how to lead a team and it was obvious they were not going to be lead by him.

We had no confidence in him as leader, so therefore we had no respect for him. He had a very bland personality and staff would come to me and tell me what he was having them do. I soon just got tired of it all and began telling them I would take care of it.

You see, he would always threaten to write them up, but he would tell me that because I began fighting back. He knew that the supervisor and the commander both had no confidence in him. We did get another med-tech on board and he was now strictly admin. The new med-tech was organized and the staff saw his leadership abilities and *we quickly took to him. He was actually a delight to work for. After the first one, I guess anyone would have been.*

I did have the opportunity to talk to the first med-tech as he was leaving the ship. Evidently, he thought I was the only who tried to show him some respect (little did he know) and he was thanking me. Then he told me something that I already knew, that he has never been able to make friends and no one as ever really liked him.

My first thought was, ya think! So you see he was a jerk but that is all he really knew how to be. So, is he really a jerk? I did try to help him, but it was like I was talking in a foreign language. I never saw or heard from him again.

This storyteller has already outlined many of the failing grades this supervisor earns. He fails to meet any of the positive traits of a good manager/leader. This manager will not accept other's ideas. He treats his subordinates as robots who should perform on his command.

Although you can personally feel sorry for someone with his poor self-esteem, it is no excuse for his lack of respect for others. Because he has no self-respect, he shows little respect for his workers. The sad thing is that he knows it, yet does nothing to change his ways.

Episode # 40

Once again, we have a military situation. This military supervisor lacks any personal concern for his troops. He was not trustworthy and is unreliable. Sometimes people get to higher ranks just because they have been there for a long time.

Of course, when it comes to promoting incompetent people, the military is no different from civilian companies. Many companies promote on seniority alone, and we know that can be a big problem.

I've worked for many jerk-managers in my military career. The one that stands out the most, was my very first supervisor at my first duty station. He was a total jerk when it came to taking care of his Soldiers.

He would pride himself on the work that we did, but wouldn't give us any credit for it. We weren't allowed as much down-time as other Soldiers. There is one time in particular that had me steaming. We were preparing to go to a field exercise, so that meant we had to load up all of our equipment.

All of the Soldiers came to work prepared to move a lot of equipment. However, we did not know how much! While he ran an errand, he told us to load the truck with all of the equipment that we would need for the exercise.

Immediately, the older Soldiers knew that meant he wasn't
going to help us load anything. I was brand new to the unit, so I did
what I was told and that was it. His instructions were very vague, as a
matter of fact there was only one instruction: "load the equipment into
this truck." We did just that. We waited and waited for him to come
back and release us for the day.

When he arrived he was not happy. He yelled and screamed and
told us how incompetent we were at completing a simple task. He
wanted the equipment that was already loaded into the truck taken off
and reloaded according to his load plan. It had taken us all of five hours
to properly package everything up and load it, but he wanted it done
his way.

I sat down and cried. All of the hard work we did while he was
gone all day had gone to waste. Everyone else in the unit was getting
released for the day and we had to do double the work. He asked me why
I was crying and I told him. Before I could get anything out, he
automatically assumed I was crying because I didn't want to do any
work.

He called me lazy and every name under the sun that you could
call a Soldier. I had to stand there and listen; when he finished I asked
him if I could tell him why I was upset. He told me it didn't matter, but
he let me tell him anyway. I told him that if he would have given us his
load plan in the beginning, we wouldn't be doing double work in the
middle of darkness. He caught a bigger fit.

What he didn't realize was that being my first supervisor, it was his job to start to shape my career path. He was supposed to lead and guide me in the right direction, so that one day I would become a great supervisor.

Needless to say, I did learn from him, but it wasn't anything good. I learned how "not" to treat my Soldiers and how to be thorough in my work habits because another Soldier may be following my footsteps thinking this is the right path to follow.

Crying out of total frustration, because of an attack on a person's character, is not a sign of weakness. In this case, the supervisor was totally uncaring about his soldier's feelings. He lashed out at them instead of taking responsibility for his failure to give proper instructions, and for not being available to supervise the work.

Management cannot abdicate the responsibility for things that go wrong. The obligation always rests on the person who gives the orders.

True leaders are always available to serve their followers. Too bad most jerk-mangers feel that their subordinates are only there to serve them.

Episode # 41

Not only does the following boss show total disrespect for his employees, he also has no appreciation for what his dental patients think of his attitude.

It is no surprise that he cannot get anyone to work for him for very long. The chances are he is not even a good dentist. Would you continue to go to a dentist with his maniacal behavior?

I worked for a boss at a local dental office. He was horrible to all the employees. He would throw instruments at the assistants, yell at them in front of patients, and talk to them like they were dirt beneath his shoes.

I had been working there for about 18 months when I decided to go back to school. I drove from school to work every day. I asked to come in on Tuesday and Thursday mornings around 10:00am. I also asked if I could take an extra 30 minutes for lunch on Mondays and Wednesdays so I could take a lunch class. He told me that if I couldn't work the whole day, then I couldn't work at all. The only day I would have been able to work was on Fridays.

When I turned in my 2 week notice, he had the nerve to ask me why I couldn't work on Fridays because I didn't have class. I kindly explained to him that if he couldn't work with me and my school schedule, I couldn't work with him and his childlike behavior and temper tantrums.

This tyrant lost a good worker because of his inexcusable juvenile behavior. Managers who let their negative emotions overrule common sense inflict pain without any remorse.

Does it make sense to lose her services for the whole day rather than for an extra half-hour time off to improve her education? His lack of compassion for his assistant's personal needs led to losing a good employee for no good reason.

Episode # 42

This storyteller seems to indicate this was the worst supervisor he or she ever had. Obviously, the feelings of being unappreciated and unworthy evoked strong feelings in this employee.

There are certain traumas in life that call for extra understanding and caring. In this case, this supervisor comes across as cold-hearted and completely uncaring.

In the late 1980s and the early 1990s, I had the questionable privilege to observe the worst supervisor I have ever known. This man supervised a group of highly technical IT resources in a very sophisticated computer center for a large multi-state company.

One story sums up the poor management behavior of this supervisor. One day, his most experienced systems programmer requested a week's leave of absence to attend her only brother's funeral in California. He was 48 years old and had experienced a sudden fatal heart attack the night before.

This employee had been incarcerated with her family in one of the Japanese camps in California during World War II. She had subsequently lost both of her parents, leaving her brother as her only family member.

After explaining the situation to her supervisor she was shocked at his response. The supervisor denied her request because she had no vacation available and would be taking unpaid leave. He then stated "What's the big deal anyway? Everyone has to die sometime." He was cut in a downsizing effort six months later.

This manager certainly does not appreciate the value in the saying: *"Blessed those who mourn; they shall be comforted."* By denying her the opportunity to go to the funeral, he certainly did not give any comfort to his employee.

Today, most companies have personnel policies that allow for family leave. The emphasis is on being with the family at an important time for grieving friends and relatives. Paid or unpaid is not the question in the minds of the bereaving workers at times like this.

Can you believe the lack of compassion is this guy? Not only did he make no accommodations for his employee to attend the funeral, his comment about people dying was totally irresponsible.

Perhaps this manager does not have any close relatives, or at least relatives that still acknowledge him.

Chapter Seven

Organizing Skills

Finally, employees expect good management skills from their superiors. Once again, I divide these expectations into these sub-categories: 1) Organizing Skills, 2) Directing Skills, and 3) Control Skills.

Organizing skills include, Good General and Job Specific Knowledge, People and Organizational Skills, Provides Effective Training and Impartial Evaluations.

Episode # 43

One of the primary reasons why jerk-managers exhibit jerk-behavior is because they are unprepared to handle the job of management. The business world is full of unqualified persons in management.

When managers are not good organizers, they remain confused, and sometimes react harshly toward their workers in response to the chaos they themselves cause.

Unfortunately, in business there are managers and leaders in positions that they are not really qualified for. There are a few ways this happens. One is that they are hired based on education only and they meet the criteria needed for the job. It is assumed that they will be a good leader.

Another way this happens is through good old fashion politics. People politic their way into positions that they are not qualified for. Another reason you might find a manager or leader in a position that they are not capable to handle is that they may have been put there as a favor to someone else.

I have seen all of these in real life and it is very hard to continue to work hard to climb the ladder the right way. I will say that these situations usually do correct themselves, but it may be too late in some circumstances.

This story could also have been listed in Chapter Three under Personal Assets. You cannot be a successful manager or leader simply by reading a book or getting a degree. It takes more than that. It takes Street Smarts too.

In the book, Wake up! Wise up! Win!, the *Street Smart Management* theory states that good managers need to have a combination "X" style management, "Y" style management and Street-Smart Management skills to be successful.

Many great leaders have little or no college education, yet the have strong Street-Smarts.

Episode # 44

It is sad but true; many mangers just cannot make difficult decisions. This shows up clearly in their inability to organize people into the right job, at the right time, in the right place.

The following story is about a whimp when it comes to making decisions.

My boss said, "You hire incompetent people to hire competent people to do the work; that's called job security." Believe it or not, I'm still trying to locate the university, governmental training programs, or even the trade school that he actually attended, because I think that we would all pass there with flying colors.

With that being said, working under his managerial philosophies were actually eye openers for m. Especially, when it came to realizing that there are a lot of people that are willing to compromise their own integrity and morals, in order to maintain employment within a dysfunctional organization.

Within the 2 years that I worked within that facility, I experienced a lot of questionable situations that really had me wondering and questioning my schooling, training, and intelligence.

For example, I was required to submit a performance appraisal that was composed of both my duties and the Budget and Administration Officer's duties.

When I refused to submit this to the head office, he called me into his office and asked me why I refused to be a team player. I point blank told him that I'm tired of doing work for other people and not getting the credit for it; case in point was when he asked me to create a slide show presentation that consisted of a thermometer with a ringing red phone and various graphic designs within a certain timeframe. I accomplished the task, and then I was informed by the Budget and Administration Officer that I had to give her my slides, and that she'll present it to the managers with my boss.

My heart sank to the pit of my stomach, because I wasn't expecting my hard work to be taken away and passed off as someone else's work.

Shortly, after this incident, my position was temporarily eliminated due to budget cuts. However, the position was reinstated within two months after I was rehired by the other contracting company that I worked for before becoming the Administrative Assistant for the first company. I consider my time working under the jerk as a lesson learned and an experience that I can share when it comes to working for a "JERK".

It appears that this administrator was calling on this employee to do the work of others in other job positions within the company. Most people do not mind doing extra work on a sometimes basis.

It can be harmful when other people take credit for the work that you are doing. This is especially distressing if the person you are doing the work for gets a higher pay than you do.

Teamwork calls for everyone to help others in times of trouble. On the contrary, when the organization is always in trouble, the main trouble could be that some of the employees are not doing their own work.

Episode # 45

The following case study is an illustration of a person "cutting his nose off to spite his face." Again, vindictiveness in any degree is a formula for managerial disaster.

Good managers try to work with their employees in any way they can to handle personal problems that come up away from work.

I used to be an assistant manager at a large theater chain, and one of the people that I worked with used to be one of those "jerk" managers. He was put in charge of the schedule and when anyone needed a certain day off, he would cut their hours back for that week.

For example if an employee wanted Thursday off next week, he would schedule them one to two days less. He'd say, "O if they need that day then they must not want to work much next week". I never understood that.

We had over 80 employees, all with rotating schedules and it literally made no difference, but that didn't matter. His whole attitude was that whole world owed him something.

The above story describes a foolishly vindictive person. He reacts as a child getting revenge. He is like a bully on the playground. In street-talk, we would say he was a "control freak." Once again, we see a lack of integrity and loyalty.

He makes decisions based on emotions and not on the business situation. This jerk lacks self-esteem and self-confidence and covers it up with spiteful control.

Self-confident people do not have to go around bragging to everyone about how great they are. Self-confident people do not worry about what others think of them.

Since early in my own career, I have known that of the secrets to becoming successful in business is to work for the smartest and most capable person I could find. They recognize competency, and they are not afraid of their subordinates. Self-confident managers give good employee evaluations.

On the other side of the coin, I have always tried to hire the smartest and most capable employees I could afford. They do good work for as long as you can continue to offer them opportunities for advancement. When they move on to bigger and better positions, I am happy for them. I did the same thing in my management career.

Episode # 46

Along with poor insight into how to plan and organize the actual work, this manager lacks people skills, the ability to direct his employees, and in the end, has little control.

Managers who give "lip service" to their employees do not encourage their employees to participate in making decisions. Employees who feel they are wasting their time usually do not waste their time making suggestions.

So, what specifically makes my "boss" a poor manager and not a great leader? Although the list is long, I will list just a few of the main things that push my buttons: My "boss" will routinely ask an opinion on issues directly within the purview of your daily work, but then blatantly disregard your input and implement an often predetermined or simply "bad" course of action.

My "boss" does not get fully engaged enough to really understand contractual requirements. Consequently, the client's expectations are ever changing and usually increasing.

It is supremely difficult to hit a moving target, and he becomes a significant generator of internal and external friction. My "boss" is socially awkward. Any sort of communication or camaraderie is difficult at best.

My "boss" is strong in the area of task organization, but has no clue when it comes to physical execution. In other words, he can put together a step-by-step list, but his orchestration of the working elements to accomplish the end-state task is often fractured and ineffective.

Insight (meaning I shouldn't know this but I do) My "boss" still holds his position only because he meets a set of very narrow hiring pre-requisites not readily available within the pool of applicants in or willing to reside here. I am confident and informed in stating my "boss" remains my "boss" not as a result of his ability to both perform personally or motivate his subordinates to achieve and exceed the client's expectations, but because there are no qualified candidates willing or available to replace him.

Hopefully these snapshots provide enough of a case for my "boss" to be classified as a poor "manager" and not a "leader." It is for these and many other reasons not listed, I consider leaving my job daily!

The above story reminds me of a time when I worked for the owner of a company who had a large round table in his office. He would have an executive meeting and start it off by saying that there was no head spot at a round table, so everyone could say what they wanted to say.

Unfortunately, he never listened to what they said, and in the end, he filed for bankruptcy a year after I left his company. Some people delude themselves into thinking they know it all.

Episode # 47

Most employees like to have some order in their lives. Knowing what the company expects of them gives employees a sense of security by knowing they are doing their jobs and that they are appreciated.

This narrative is a perfect example of a manager who has no concept of how to organize her workforce effectively.

I don't know if being a really bad manager makes someone a jerk, but I once worked for this lady that refused to schedule people for more than a day in advance. I had to call in every morning to see if she needed me to work. Occasionally, she would be able to make a decision before I would leave the previous day. Yeah, that got really old, really fast.

She was a nice person, but her managing skills were really awful.

Working is this type of topsy-turvy environment is hard on the employees and hard on their families. Just being a "nice" person does not make for a good manager.

Good managers not only know how to schedule, they also know how the schedule will affect their employees' family lives. All work and no play is not good for anyone.

Episode # 48

Sometimes, bosses think they have the power to be leaders just because they are the "boss." They are sadly mistaken.

A leader's power comes from those who are willing to follow them. All too often, people get promoted to positions that require leadership, when they actually have little or no leadership ability at all. This is a monumental problem in corporate America.

Another issue that contributes to a jerk manager would be the ones who think being bossy is the same as leadership. Manager cannot do it all alone. Therefore you must delegate out tasks to your employees.

When doing this the proper way, you would delegate out the tasks and inform each member the priority of each tasks to be completed. From there you should notify them of any known potential issues they may have.

112

Afterwards, during a reasonable time make a follow up to get a progress report of the tasks at hand.

It appears this boss has very little understanding of when and how to delegate effectively. A manager who cannot determine who is able to handle delegated authority will generally not delegate authority without micro-management. They feel they are the only ones who can do the job right, and they need to control everything.

Working under this type of ill-prepared boss is very hard on the self-esteem needs of the employees. Bosses who make their employees feel incompetent to handle a job make their employees feel unappreciated and unwanted.

Everyone needs to feel some form of love and acceptance to perform at that best.

Chapter Eight

Directing Skills

Simply because there is no distinct starting and stopping point for each of the three management skills we study, it is difficult to separate the functions of management. They truly overlap and in the words of the old song about love and marriage, *"you can't have one without the others."*

Nevertheless, we will try to look at directing skills to include the ability to solve problems and make effective decisions.

Episode # 49

This story is short and not so sweet. However, it is indicative of many conditions in small organizations, where *"who you know"* is more important than *"what you know."*

In any walk of life, people who feel that they are invincible make life difficult for everyone else. They tend to run roughshod over their underlings.

People, who build their self-worth relying on who they know, are generally personally devastated when the person who protects them dies, retires, or just gets tired of covering for them.

Yes, I had a boss whom I considered a jerk. This particular boss nothing pleased her. She did not have any managerial skills at all. She was the boss because of her relationship with the doctor (her friend).

I think, because she didn't know or understand her position, she got a kick out of making everyone else's life miserable.

The narrator certainly has no good words for this boss. There are people out there who find pleasure in making others miserable. This is perhaps the worst kind of person to work under.

Actually, this boss appears to have a very poor personal opinion of her own self. Evidently, she believes that since she does not deserve respect, she need not show respect for anyone else. Perhaps, the reason she is able to remain in the job is because the business owner has the same problem she has.

This is explanation describes a common situation in many small professional businesses. It can also be true when a doctor, dentist or other professional has his or her spouse running the office.

Nepotism is not necessarily bad in itself. Nepotism is bad when is generates special treatment for the related employees and negative treatment for the other people in the organization.

People who delight in making others miserable are usually miserable people. It is the same old condition, which causes gossip and vandalism. "If I can't be happy, why should others?" "If I can't have something, why should you?"

Evidently, this oppressor has never heard: *Blessed are the peacemakers.* Because she has no inner peace, she makes sure none of her employees has any peace at work. She makes life miserable for everyone else.

Happy people have no reason to make others unhappy. In fact, happy people do not even like being around grumpy people. Happy people want to enjoy life and have fun.

Episode # 50

There is an art to tactful communication. Encouragement is much more effective than condemnation. This journal entry clearly shows why nagging is unproductive.

Good communication is a two-way street. It involves both sending and receiving messages. One-way communication is a sign of a closed mind.

Several of the managers that I worked for that I found to be jerk-managers were micro managers. This is because they would nitpick at every single detail, even if you did a majority of your tasks right.

117

In such cases, I found myself unmotivated to do much to the best of my ability, for the reason that my managers would never recognize what I did well, but rather what I did wrong.

Sometimes, they would not even give me a reason as to why the job was unsuitable. So, I did not know how to fix my faults or even what they were for that matter. I find positive managers to be far more effective and make for a more happy set of employees.

It is safe to say that most employees certainly want to work in a pleasant atmosphere. Since we spend most of our waking time at work, does it make sense that we want to enjoy the time?

This employee indicates she did not do her best work because she was unhappy. However, do all unhappy workers do poor work? We do not really know. What we do know is that we will never know how much better quality work and more productivity unhappy workers could do if they were happy.

Episode # 51

Diversity is the name of the game in today's business world. Partiality and harassment causes undue turmoil in the workplace.

Managers who do not appreciate the wealth of experience that diverse workers bring to the table are missing out on the great value of diversity.

I think that one thing managers can do to avoid being a jerk is treat ALL employees fairly. I worked at a restaurant in 2001, and the manager purposely gave me the most work so he could hang out with the rest of his guy employees and his girlfriend, which I thought was very selfish and just plain dumb.

What makes a good manager is a person not afraid of doing working or helping others even if it's not within their job description, because I feel that this is where a person's title is earned not just given.

The writer did not make it clear if the girlfriend was also an employee. That would have only made the situation worse. Plainly, her boss did favor the other male employees. Gender discrimination is still alive and well in many workplaces.

Sadly, some men still feel that women are second-class employees. It becomes illegal when men consider their female employees to be a fair target for sexual innuendoes or unwanted advances.

Of course, we can say the same thing about all other types of discrimination in the workplace. Some of the best ideas for improving the companies I have managed came from workers who could not read or write. They were some of the most productive workers we had.

Episode # 52

Just as in business, positions of power in the military are not a sure sign of managerial capability. Whether in civilian or military life, many people attain higher positions simply through seniority.

Although promotions due to seniority are not problematic in themselves, many times they are a problem because of the individual person promoted, not because of the promotion system.

Jerk Bosses are something of an art in the US .... I don't know if it is the pressures of command or the ever shrinking supply of capable managers and leaders. In my short 4 and half years as an officer (with the experience of 6 years on active duty as a Non-Commissioned Officer and 4 years in the Reserves, I have run across a few gems as "jerk" bosses.

One commander of mine was a compassionless jerk. Now the military is run simply by what is good for the "unit", the higher organization, the good for the whole. While I was deployed overseas, my wife; also an officer, was deployed at the same time. It turned out that her job title was cut from our unit and assigned to another one across the river, about 6 miles away.

It was a very long, dangerous 6 miles, and in 6 months of being deployed we saw each other once. Finally, my unit was on the down side of an operational phase and there truly was not a lot going on.

My unit was performing the mission as always, and I had an opportunity to take a day or so and see my wife. When I asked my boss about it he simply said, " I can't see my wife, you can't see yours."

I was livid, and distraught. His wife was at home, and she was a friend of my wife and caring for her and her three children. My wife on the other hand was across the river, braving insurgent attacks, roadside bombs, and all manner of horrible potential death. (My wife earned a Bronze Star and Combat Action Badge for her efforts in the war) Every moment to us was precious, but it was stopped cold by the illogic of a compassionless jerk.

Luckily, her boss was not a jerk. (As I side note, this boss contacted me recently.. 18months or so after the time we spent together and apologized for being a jerk and a bad boss, praising us (me and my fellow lieutenants) for our hard work and contributions to our unit's success.

I appreciated it, the military is a small place and you never know when your old boss is in a position to help you out, never burn a bridge. All that aside he was still a jerk.

Currently I serve under a jerk, he just has zero understanding of human dynamics other than give me what I want. The stresses of senior command are manifold and constant and being in a place without a family but there is little excuse for this level of jerkiness.

Constantly during Staff meetings, he will say "everything would be ok if you just did what I told you to do." Never was there a time where he was willing to help his officers. He wanted us to do anything he told us to do, just because he said it was so.

Understanding that the people who work for you are human, with human wants and human needs is paramount to good leadership. "Your people will make you or break you" is an old slogan. It is certainly still true in the world today. The role of a leader is to serve the people he or she leads. When it comes to lacking the ability to direct the people under their control, jerk-officers are just as bad as jerk-managers.

You can have the best equipment or armament in the world, and if you do not have the right people using it, you have nothing.

Episode # 53

Everyone makes mistakes from time to time. Yet, without a doubt, not allowing your employees to make mistakes is the poorest decision a responsible manager can make.

Poor productivity is the normal outcome when a manager does not have the self-confidence to let their employees make mistakes.

I have been some sort of manager since I was 16, working at McDonalds was my start. Along the way I have learned a lot of lessons, some easy and some hard.

The best thing that I learned from the worst manager that I ever had is how not to treat people. As a manager now, I remember everyday how it felt to have been belittled and threatened to be let go from my job for what to me seemed to be for no reason at all. I truly respect the people that I have working for me, and I do my best to be open, honest, and fair to each of them.

The most valuable lesson I have learned is that people work for people, not companies.

While many companies require a college degree to get ahead in today's corporate world, just having a degree does not translate into being capable. In this case, this supervisor refused to back up his employees when they made decisions for him.

As in this case, a reputation for being untrustworthy is hard to defuse. No one trusts a person who lacks a backbone when it comes to accepting responsibility. Employees expect their managers to have integrity.

Episode # 54

Giving direction does not mean giving constant negative criticism. Bosses who micro-manage by demeaning and degrading their employees' work performance seldom improve their employees' performance. Attacking a person's self-confidence is not the way to encourage anyone.

This detailed report gives a graphic illustration of the problem with a jerk micro-manager.

I have a total of over ten years in the banking world and have had many wonderful bosses, and a few who were true jerk-managers. The biggest jerk for a boss maintained a personality of a criticizer and a micromanager. Below is an outline of what made her the biggest jerk that I ever worked for.

My employment at a large Credit Union .Job Title -Utility Teller -responsible for maintaining and balancing ATM machines located in the area. Deposits and withdrawals averaged 200 to 400 thousand daily. Only 2 days for training was allowed in my new position. I was constantly on call for emergencies (failures) of ATM machines.

First Issue

Only been at credit union for 1.5 months when a member asked me to send a CUMO.

I rarely worked front desk and was not familiar with this term or procedure. Had no previous training on CUMO. I went to her door was locked (as usual). She provided an instruction sheet on how to send a CUMO.

I realized that I did not have access to the screens listed on the instruction sheet and informed the member that I would have to ask someone else to send it.

Every representative was assisting someone, so I went back to her and told her that I could not send it. Before I could tell her that I did not have access to certain screens, she grabs the paper...sits behind my desk and in front of the customer states, "It's not difficult.. .can't you follow directions?"

I apologized to the customer for the delay and was truly insulted and hurt by the words and behavior of my manager.

Second and Last Issue

I worked for credit union for 6 months now no work issues. I had chosen to avoid this supervisor and became an introvert and focused only on my work and the members. Wednesday morning around 9:30 am – She opens the door to the ATM vault and says, "I'm going to have to write you up."

I was dumbfounded and asked, "For what?" She states, "Monday's deposit was $50.00 short." I replied, "I balanced, I have all of the copies from that deposit...here they are. I don't understand, yes, the deposit was large...but I know I balanced. Has a member claimed their deposit was wrong?" She says, "No, the teller at Main office and did not balance and she processed your work."

I asked, "Do they have her teller audit sheet? If I compare my teller work with her work.. maybe I could locate her shortage." Boss tells me, "No, that won't be necessary...everything points to the ATM deposit."

I asked for an opportunity to reconcile Monday's deposit.. She tells me that I would have to do it by Friday (close of business)..."You are not going to get me in trouble...if it's not found by Friday I will write you up."

My day off was on Thursday. I had to try to reconcile the huge deposit from Monday while working as scheduled on a super busy Friday. Monday's deposit was over $23 K in cash, $89 K in checks and over $133 K in withdrawals.

Friday came -I managed to reconcile the deposit over my one-hour lunch break. I went over the deposit 3 times and could not locate any errors. The deposit was correct when it was picked up by the security guard in the armored car.

I was confused and decided to tell her that I could not find where the deposit was short, and that it was in full balance when it left the vault. After, getting her attention away from her computer...I proceed to tell her that I did not find the $50.00 shortage and would only sign a warning if I was able to make a rebuttal statement and submit proof for my rebuttal.

She looks down at the computer and mumbles, "Oh, you're safe this time. The branch manager found the $50.00...the teller had miscounted." I said, "Good, but when where you going to tell me?" She still does not look at me and only says, "It's over now."

I left her office and immediately and documented the whole incident. What kind of jerk would allow an employee to stress over an issue that had been resolved and not even apologize for the immediate assumption that they made toward their own employee being a thief?

Not to mention, the jerk could care less about her employee missing lunch because she did not bother to tell the employee the money had been found. Oh, by the way the teller who was $50.00 short only got a verbal warning.

I found out later that a written warning was only applicable to a shortage or overage of more than $100 dollars but my boss was going to write me up when it was only $50.00.

On Monday morning I applied for a transfer that would also be considered a promotion. I was promoted within 3 weeks and worked at the main office as a member-service representative.

I was selected as employee of the month twice in 1998 and was awarded Member Service Representative of the year in 1998. Other promotions came while I was employed there I was promoted to the credit card department, then as a telecommuter for the credit union (which I worked out of my own home for 9 months). I stayed with the credit union until I moved to another job.

I never complained against the jerky boss until my exit interview. I showed HR my documentation and made other suggestions as to how to improve the work environment.

I went back to visit friends a few years later and did see one of my suggestions enacted (hiring a part time teller on busy days because the work volume was increasing month by month, especially on Mondays, Tuesday and Fridays). She was still there and I waved but did not speak to her.

I learned that she would not change so I had to either adapt to her way or find a way to get out of the environment. I also learned that personality types should truly be considered when putting a person into a management position. She had no human interaction skills and no humor. Work was her life and her employees avoided her at all cost, almost as though she had the plague.

I vowed to never treat another employee like this. Before I decided to write someone up I would inquire about the situation and listen to both sides.

There are so many reasons why this manager is a jerk it is hard to know where to start. Obnoxious personal traits, few personal skills, hardly any people skills, and a complete lack of management skills all fit the circumstances with this manager.

Rash judgment is only a part of this supervisor's failure at proper direction. Good managers make sure of the facts before they start blaming people. Placing blame is not the way to solve a business problem. Finding the cause of a problem is the proper course before taking any action.

Episode # 55

The last essay in this chapter outlines a problem in directing. It results from a complete lack of understanding of the job at hand. Managers need to know what they need to know.

Managers who are in over their heads have a tough time staying afloat on their own, let alone giving effective directions to others.

Changing thoughts now, I had to work on a project at which they put a recent college grad in charge of as the Project Manager. He had no skills, did not know how to communicate, could not express his desires or goals, and did not know the infrastructure we were working in; but he made the triple digit salary because he had the latest and greatest insight because he just graduated with his MBA from college.

He was the worst PM I ever worked with, and he failed miserably in everything he did, but he kept getting promoted because of the money they had invested in him, and he graduated from the same school as out VP.

He could not even carry on an intelligent conversation one-on-one, and was a JERK to everyone because he knew he was in over his head and everyone else had to bail him out, or look bad ourselves.

Evidently, this essay writer still has some strong negative feelings about this former boss. Many competent employees carry the load for their incompetent bosses. Alas, many situations like this exist in business. However, it should not be that way.

Again, this is a case of *"book learnin"* being insufficient to insure this person can do the job. Project management requires understanding the job at hand, the conditions involved in completing the job, and the ability to keep abreast of the project as it progresses.

In this case, the project manager gets protection for political reasons, not for good performance. Obviously, if his employees are covering for him, his boss might think he is doing great.

Of course, the worst alternative could be to let the project manager fall on his face. However, it is highly possible that everyone could be a loser in that case.

Chapter Nine

Controlling Skills

Control skills come under the final list of basic qualifications employees expect of a leader. They include effective follow-up efforts and accountability.

Within the functions of management, failure to follow-up on plans after implementation is a common problem. Problems do not usually solve themselves.

Episode # 56

One of the basic functions of organizational control facing most managers is the task of scheduling. Keeping abreast of the overall requirements for human resources is at the heart of good management.

Managers who give no thought to the personal side of their workers' lives make it difficult for their workers to be satisfied with their jobs.

One of the first two jobs that I had was one where you apply for the job by filling out the times and days that you are available to work.

First of all, I was still in high school, so it was usually evenings and weekends. The original manager who hired me was promoted, so this JERK took over. He was horrible at making the weekly workshift schedule. He would schedule me on Saturday from 8 to 1 and the next person wouldn't be on the schedule until 3 pm.

So when the store was busy (most of the time because it was near the airport) he would ask me to stay until the next person came in, because he did not want to come down to work on the floor. He wanted to stay in his office. I actually told him that he was bad at scheduling and if he wasn't going to pay me overtime then I would no longer stay to assist.

In the end I won that battle. He probably thought I was a JERK.

The essay does not tell us whether the manager improved his scheduling skills or gave the writer overtime pay. However, if the worker is upset having to work late every Saturday, then getting paid for overtime does not really solve the problem.

One of a manager's jobs is to meet their employees' basic human needs. One of those human needs an employee has is a social life away from work.

All employees need understanding for their human needs. Managers who do not allow for such personal needs fall short when it comes to this truism: *Blessed are the merciful.* We need to show mercy in the little things as well as in times of a crisis.

Expecting young workers to have total dedication to a part-time job is unrealistic. Because he could not put himself in this young worker's shoes, chances are he thought his worker was a jerk.

Episode # 57

Because it tells of the case of a supervisor who mends his jerkish ways, this tale has a happy ending. Sad that it does not happen often enough.

The story does show us that it is always important to stand up for what you believe.

When I was a sophomore in high school, I began working at an Italian restaurant. I began as a hostess in the busiest store in the nationwide chain. As a result, many evenings were extremely hectic with rude customers and overbearing, stressed managers.

I was terrified of the proprietor (manager), because of his strict no-nonsense attitude on the job. I was so intimidated by him when I first started that I would walk clear around the opposite side of the restaurant to avoid his line of sight.

One night I was working with the head hostess when she left the podium with the master seating chart to take care of something quickly. After she left, a large table had opened, making perfect accommodations for the party of eight that had been waiting over an hour to be seated.

I made the executive decision to seat the large party at that table while the head hostess was away from the scene. Upon seating the party, I made my way to the back kitchen. While in the kitchen, unbeknownst to me, management became irate with my decision to seat the party.

Apparently there was a miscommunication and some secretive guests were supposed to be seated before the party that had been waiting patiently over an hour.

So while I was rolling silverware in the kitchen my boss proceeded to lecture me in a very disrespectful tone. He said, 'What are you stupid?!" and I could not take it after that. I stood up to him for the first time and yelled back, explaining my decision and reasons why. I think he was surprised that I had an opinion in the matter, and every day after that point he acted impressed with me and my work ethic.

I think he needed to see that I wasn't weak in order to respect me and not be such a jerk with his mentoring.

Calling an employee stupid is about as unfeeling as you can get. It is a personal attack. Luckily, the young employee stood up for herself, and she told him what she thought of his mentoring. In these circumstances, most young employees are not prepared to stand up for themselves.

The good part about this story is that the boss changed his attitude. Sometimes, bosses just don't realize the effect they have on their subordinates.

Episode # 58

While not all micro-managers are jerk-managers, when it comes to control issues, all micro-managers have a problem with over-control. This narrator points out that very problem.

Micro-managers stunt the growth of their employees, and hinder their empowerment and ability to handle greater responsibility.

Well the issue with micro-managers is they do not know the line in between valuing the skills of the employee and motivating them for new things. They sometimes fail to realize the repetitiveness in the particular task(s) and the fact that the employee has done it numerous times.

Follow ups should probably be used versus spending time giving out details on a project in which the standard quality expectations and tasks of the position are always the same. It would allow for more time to get it done, instead of learning about the situation which is a normal issue that always gets resolved.

Perhaps this micro-manager was not really a jerk. Nevertheless, the writer believes that he was. At least for the employee, perception is what counts.

Too much oversight brings on frustration. People do not appreciate hearing the same thing repeatedly. It makes them feel rejected and unworthy. It harms their self-confidence and self-esteem.

In any case, we can see that this boss's micro-management is making this employee feel less than valuable to the organization.

Episode # 59

The street-name for this tyrant-in-charge would be "control freak." Not only did he keep tabs on everything his workers did, he took credit for anything they did well.

It is common for this type of micro-manager to have his or her supervisor fooled into thinking that they were doing a great job, when all along it was the workers performing effectively in spite of the manager.

I have worked for plenty of jerk-managers in my young life. The jerk of this story is no stranger to being called a jerk. I know he has heard it numerous amounts of times, because I've heard it in his presence! Jerk wasn't the exact term they used, but it was pretty close.

For the purposes of this story, he was an intermediate supervisor; he led teams of 15 and under. Within his team there were team leaders. Believe me when I tell you "Team Leader" was just a title, it was.

We had no control of our team members or our tasks. We were completely micromanaged. If we received a task and met the deadline, the work may have gotten compliments from our big boss, but not from him. He would accept the credit for the work and come back and down us constantly.

The big boss didn't know what was happening besides the fact that our supervisor said we had poor performance and that he had to always fix everything. Our performance counseling reports reflected his attitude toward us.

We complained but he had the big boss fooled. It wasn't until he had to go on convalescent leave after a surgery that the big boss realized it was our work all along and he had been giving the credit to the wrong person.

For that month our office ran smoothly and the big boss had absolutely no complaints. We finally received the acknowledgement that we deserved. When he came back he was in for a big surprise.

The big boss had promoted two team leaders and given us our own sections. We were now his peers and he had new fish to swindle. He was under review for almost six months before the big boss call him

out and told him about his poor behavior and negative energy. He was
ultimately demoted and later fired.

    Although it was hard as a team leader under the jerk, I learned
what type of leader not to become. That experience taught me that we
have to pick and choose our own battles. Complaining gets you
nowhere, but patience is a silent killer!

    Yes, we must admit that most jerk-managers do eventually get their justly deserved comeuppance. The trouble is, sometimes it takes a long time. These employees had to suffer through his dictatorial attitude long before he finally met his demise from higher management.

    It seems that this micro-managing jerk enjoyed his reputation as a jerk. He even took out his insecurity by giving his employees poor performance evaluations. Managers with mediocre skills do not recognize good performance when the see it.

Episode # 60

    This chronicler weaves a similar tale to the one we just looked at. It is about another manager with no leadership ability.

It never ceases to amaze me that so many people with poor leadership ability are in so many important management roles.

There is a huge difference between a "leader" and a "manager". Leaders have the ability to transform potential into reality by influencing their subordinates to voluntarily meet and often exceed some predefined objective.

Managers, on the other hand, are little more than figureheads achieving marginal results through planned activities, organization of meaningless structures, and loose control of resources.

Fortunately, the vast majority of the "bosses" I have worked for would fit nicely in the category of leader; however, I currently work for a very poor manager. At my place of business, there is no vision or inspiration.

My boss has never demonstrated the willingness to stretch himself beyond his normal capabilities, and there is no protection from expanding non-contractual requirements.

It is for these reasons and the few others I will discuss during the remainder of this paper, my current boss can be classified as solidly in the managerial pool and somewhat of a "Jerk" to work for.

In my opinion, the worst trait a boss can exhibit is the inability to understand the requirement and the defined obligation enough to tell the client "no." When you find yourself in a work environment with an ever expanding responsibility but no additional resources or recourse to "stop the madness," frustration quickly becomes significant dissatisfaction and burnout. As a result, many organizations have significantly high turnover rates -mine included.

Over the past eleven months, three of the four positions similar to mine have either been vacant or the hires have come and gone. From the periphery, the constant turnover could easily appear as many things other than poor leadership; however, of those who filled these positions temporarily throughout the year, all have cited our "boss" as the reason for leaving the organization.

Turnover is certainly a serious problem in many companies. Most of it can be traced to the lack of leadership at the mid and low-level management positions. Of course, we have to admit that upper-management allows this to happen.

Anyone can be a manager. All it takes is someone with the authority to appoint you as a manager. Some managers rule with a clenched fist and force their workers to do their bidding.

The power of leadership on the other hand, flows upward from the people who allow you to lead them. Employees follow their leaders because they want to. Leaders lead with open hands and hearts.

Episode # 61

The disdain in this storytellers writing is clear. She shows it with the use of the word "girl." She does not even give her boss the dignity of calling her a woman.

After reading her story, you will understand why she still holds resentment toward this former supervisor.

I worked for a girl when I was in the military who was about 5 years younger than me and tow pay-grades over me.

Every day at work, she came in about 10 minutes late. She would put her bag on her desk and immediately leave to go get coffee and breakfast in the same building. After her "first break" she would come back and demand to know where her full set of maintenance reports from the previous day were. I had to hand them to her because she did not allow them to just be left on her desk, but she was always mad when she walked over to her desk that the reports were not there.

In addition, when data input was needed and maintenance customers came in, she did not deal with them. I could have 10 people in line and she would sit in direct sight of me and read a magazine.

She said she was an analyst and did not need to do those types of tasks. She would not move and often refused me a lunch break, stating "the military pays us to work 24/7." Usually about this time she would leave for lunch and be gone an additional 15-20 minutes.

At the end of the day, I was required to clean the office before leaving. I had no problem with this as I was the junior sailor. It is just the way it goes. She demanded that I clean the coffee pot and the microwave too.

I thought it was unfair for me to clean these items because I did not drink coffee or use the microwave. One day while I was cleaning, a customer came in and in accordance with good practice I stopped what I was doing and helped him. I was inputting the job order into the computer when she came back into the office and demanded to know, while the customer was there, why I was "playing with the computer instead of cleaning so we all can leave on time?"

I told her I would sweep when I finished the job order. She started screaming at me, "How dare I disrespect her!" she said if I am given a task I must finish it before I start another. I had to stop what I was doing and sweep and mop the floor, while the customer waited for me to finish. This was about 30 minutes.

Just as I was finishing the cleaning tasks, The boss came in and asked the customer how long he had been sitting there. He then asked me why I was ignoring the customer and cleaning instead of helping him. She comes raging out of the back room and tells him that I always act that way and I was just trying to get out of work early and she had no idea that the customer was waiting.

So here came another lecture from the boss about priorities of work. I worked with this girl for about 5 months with every day the same. Thank God the military sees fit to move people and I got orders to leave.

Although working for her was awful, it did come full circle. Her supervisor started to document what she was doing and 4 years ago when I was just an E-3 and as a E-5 she made life awful for me. I went back last year to Florida to visit a friend and my old co-workers and she was there. I walked in, in uniform, and she demanded to know if I had orders back there?

She then proceeded to talk down to me as usual. Good old boss walked out and tells her to stand up and be respectful when talking to a commissioned officer. It was at this time, she finally noticed I was an 0-1 and that she was now only an E-4.

She has been in trouble and lost rank. I smiled at her and told her I wished her well, and that I thought when we worked to together that she was an E-5. She turned red and I walked away.

This story epitomizes the overall problem with jerk-managers. They seldom lack only one or two positive personal traits. They lack most of them, if not all of them.

She is arrogant, lacks any people skills, has trouble communicating, is very poor at organizing tasks, lacks personal integrity and espouses a "do as I say, not as I do" attitude. All in all, the writer pegs her as a jerk of the highest magnitude.

Blessed Are The Poor In Spirit is another proven adage that good managers should follow. Self-confident managers know their abilities, yet they know that they are not the "be all and end all" in the big scheme of things in life.

In the final review, almost every one of the *Jerk-Stories* we have read tells the same sad situation. Here are important questions we need to ask. Is this is a condition that top management unwittingly fosters? Does the problem lie completely within the personalities of the jerk-mangers? Can the overall effectiveness of managers be improved by greater education?

We can hope that most ineffective managers do not wish to be jerk-managers, and with the proper guidance and care, they can change their ways. One thing is certain. jerks will only change if they want to change. We cannot make them change.

In the final chapter, we will look at the bright side of this longing that most employees have for positive leadership.

Chapter Ten

Leadership

Seeking Peak Performance

Before we finish this book, it is only fair to say that certainly not all managers are jerks. Let's take a quick look at why some employees believe their managers are true leaders and great managers.

Episode # 62

Sometimes, when we have gained more experience in life, we see things differently from how we saw them in our youth. This tale describes what wisdom can do for you.

This story teaches us a valuable lesson. While it would be great if everyone at work were friendly and likeable, we know that that is not the case. Befriending everyone and establishing a personal relationship on the job is not necessary.

Nevertheless, we do have to conduct our at-work activities in a non-threatening and impersonal manner. Compatibility within the workplace is the thing we need to achieve.

Compatibility does not mean that everybody has to be buddy-buddy. It only means that everyone on the team has to have the same work ethic. Compatibility requires equal respect and treatment for all employees, regardless of their position in the organization. Compatibility builds on the Golden Rule.

When I was in the military, I thought my immediate supervisor was a "JERK" with a capital J. As I grew older I realized that being 18 years old working on Air Craft worth hundreds of millions of dollars was a daunting task and that there was little to no room for error. I didn't fully understand why he did the things he did until I was much older.

The discipline that he helped instill in me has taken me a long way, and the military teaches that excellence is not the exception but the rule.

As a civilian I have rarely come across many managers that I couldn't work with, although I have had a few that could be considered jerk-managers. When I do cross their paths I usually concentrate on the tasks at hand and my work performance. I try to eliminate any personal relationship what so ever to avoid conflict until I or they have moved on.

Originally, this mechanic thought the supervisor was a jerk. He or she did not understand that the supervisor was standing up for what was right. He was upholding his principles of professional work.

Having piloted some of those multi-million dollar Air Force aircrafts that this storyteller talks about, I can certainly appreciate the effort this supervisor put into insuring that his workers did their best.

Sometimes it seems like less work to take the easy way out. Yet, this maintenance supervisor understood the most important requirement for people in charge of others. A supervisor's job is to insure that the workers complete the job at hand efficiently and effectively. Good managers understand that having everyone like you is not the most important thing in life. They understand this beatitude:

Blessed those persecuted in the cause of right.

Episode # 63

In this last episode about a great boss, we see convincing evidence that there are indeed good managers and leaders in this world.

I have a story about a very good boss. A boss who has provided a pleasant, challenging and rewarding job experience.

I work in an IT (Information Technology) company. It is a quiet office (with occasional jokes and laughter) with my boss and co-workers sitting and working at computers all day long. I/we also have conference calls with clients several times per week.

The attributes of my boss, which make him so good are:

Appreciative – He always says "thank you."

Supportive when I feel insecure about taking on a new task – "Don't worry, I know you can do it!"

Complementary – "You did a great job"

Flexible – Willing to listen to different points of views

Principled – Gives the client a good product and is always honest in his business dealings

Gives a good product – We provide great service for a very good price to the client

Generous – Good pay, holiday parties, perks.

He went above and beyond for me personally – I was just a part-time employee when I started with him and he personally taught me the skills for the career I now have. He was sincerely interested in me being able to do more, so that I could make more money. He makes sure to let me know that I am an asset to the company and appreciates my contribution.

He is thoughtful and careful when he hires new staff, and has assembled a great team of people, who all take our jobs seriously, yet are able to make it fun and always interesting. Our team members must collaborate on projects often, and it is always a good experience, with a good outcome for the client.

And… he is funny – has a great sense of humor, and allows us to keep a loose and pleasant atmosphere in the office.

Obviously, this boss exhibits all of the positive personal traits, along with the people and management skills expected by most employees. It is unfortunate too that all employees cannot say such good things about their bosses.

Sadly, the *Jerk-Stories* we have looked at certainly provide a vivid litany of sins committed by our jerk-managers. The task for us as managers is to understand and fulfill the expectations of our employees.

Investigating why our employees value the following positive traits in their leaders will help us gain respect for their expectations.

Personal Traits

The most important thing we need to consider in studying the positive personal traits employees expect are the employees' needs for self-preservation, safety and basic social needs. We can clearly see Maslow's Hierarchy of Needs at play in the workplace.

Each one of the 24 positive traits expected by employees relates to one or more of Maslow's five basic human needs (Maslow, 1954).

While many of the 24 traits overlap, each one has a specific place in the overall roll of positive leadership. We will look at each one individually.

Creative Vision is the essence of a manager's ability to lead their organizations into the future. Creative vision of the direction the organization is headed reduces the employees' fears of the unknown. It provides a leader's followers with a sense of safety and security for their working future.

A lack of creative vision causes employees to fear the future. They wonder, "How long will my job last?" "Do I have a future with this company?" "Will the company make it?" Employees want to have faith in their managers.

Critical Thinking Ability demonstrates a manager's skills in solving problems. The main thing that sets managers apart from their employees is the function of decision-making.

While most employees want to feel as though they can fend for themselves without over-supervision, at the same time they want good guidance from their managers. They want to trust their managers to lead them in the right direction for growth and prosperity.

There is no question that people want to trust the people who are in charge. They want their leaders to have *Good Ethics*. Socially, we need to feel secure in our relationships. If we do not trust those in charge, we will fear that we cannot rely on them personally. Again, it is a safety and social needs factor.

Loyalty to Company and Workers goes along with the need for job security. Workers understand that managers, who denigrate the company or who steal from or harm the company in any way, might also do the same to them

We achieve loyalty only on a two-way street. Disloyal jerk-managers cannot expect loyalty from their workers. Yet again, it goes back to ethics. Loyalty demands truth in our relationships.

Personal Integrity and ethics go together like love and marriage. As the old song says, "You can't have one without the other." Integrity is at the heart of all working relationships. All of us have social needs, which call for mutual trust and loyalty.

Reliability is a trait akin to ethics and integrity, yet ethical and trustworthy people can be unreliable for other reasons. Nonetheless, for whatever reason, unreliable jerk-managers cause employees to feel unimportant and unworthy. A boss that does not accept responsibility usually places blame on those he or she supervises. If you cannot rely on a person, you feel alone and rejected by that person.

Sufficiently Educated only means that the manager has enough education to do the job at hand. Formal academic education is not the entire answer. That education my come from on-the-job-training. In either case, workers need to feel their bosses know what they are doing.

The higher you go in an organization, the more knowledge you need. Line workers need to know the specific job they perform. First line supervisors need to know what their workers need to know and know how to help them perform the work they do. Higher echelon managers need to know everything taking place below their level along with how to make decisions having an effect on a wider range of company goals.

Once more, we see *Trustworthy and Trusting* as very important basic values a manager must hold. Similar to ethics, loyalty, integrity and reliability, trust is a slightly different attribute. It goes to the very essence of good personal relationships.

Some supervisors can be unethical in business activities, can appear to have no loyalty to the company, can lack integrity when it comes to dealing with customers, and can be unreliable at solving problems business problems. Yet, lack of personal trust is the most destructive trait. If they are not trustworthy and do not trust you, it signifies a negative trait that has an effect on an employee's individual and personal level.

Habitual liars are untrustworthy in everything they say. A person who is untrustworthy in little things is untrustworthy in big things too. A person, who is untrustworthy, is untrustworthy in every aspect of their being.

People Skills

There is good reason why we place personal traits at the beginning of the list of positive expectations of managers. Managers who do not possess good personal
traits will generally fail at exercising good people skills.

Why is *acknowledging good work* important? Acknowledging good work not only feeds and employee's self-esteem, it gives them a stronger sense of belonging. Bosses that provide positive feedback for good performance foster a social bonding within the group.

Conversely, employees who do not know where they stand with their bosses often times operate in a state of fear that they will lose their jobs. Job security is an important aspect of meeting human survival and safety needs.

Along the same line, employees want to feel that their supervisors are *Available to Workers*. People want to feel that they have their manager's support. They need the social interaction with the person who controls their work environment.

A manager's job is to serve the people they manage. Managers who lock themselves away from their workers have little understanding of their role as managers.

Although we have listed the desired traits of leadership in alphabetical order, *Effective Communication Skills* is an absolute must for fulfilling the rest of the expectations.

The basic manner in which a person communicates dictates how they will perform in all of the 24 positive traits expected by their employees. Good communicators generally have positive personal traits, possess good people skills and easily perform the functions of management.

Then again, without adequate communication skills, both for sending and receiving information, there is little effective guidance within the organization.

People should enjoy their work. A manager's effort to *Exhibit Friendliness* pays big dividends for teamwork. A friendly manager sets a cordial tone for the climate of the organization. Members of the group are not afraid to be friendly to each other if the boss exhibits friendliness.

Managers, who are dour and who never have a friendly word, set a negative social tone in an organization. People do not react positively to negative behavior. They can also become cynical and eventually exhibit the same negative behavior as the boss. Unfriendliness is contagious.

One of the main requirements for organizational compatibility is *Impartiality and Fairness*. Especially in today's diverse workforce, any hint of prejudicial or favored treatment is certain to cause troubles in an organization.

As we have seen in the previous *Jerk-Stories*, everyone wants fair treatment. Most employees do not want any special treatment, they just do not want unfair treatment.

Employees who feel that they excluded from the group suffer the loss of social interactions and their self-esteem is adversely affected.

Personal Support for Workers is a close ally of *being available*. All employees are human and have human problems. Employees cannot expect their managers to solve their personal problems. Nevertheless, employees do desire understanding and personal support in as much as the company can provide.

Treating employees like machines takes away their humanity. Employees need social connections at work and impersonal treatment by the boss results in harm to the employees' self-motivation and group morale.

As we clearly see, lack of *Respectability and Respect For Workers* is a problem in most of the *Jerk-Stories* we have studied. Managers who do not respect themselves have a difficult time respecting others. If they feel that they do not deserve respect, then they have no desire to respect others.

Respect is definitely a two-way proposition. If you do not give respect, you will not receive respect in return. Managers do not have to be loved by or love their employees. They do need to respect their workers and get respect from the workers. Everyone deserves respect.

Finally, when it comes to people skills, *Shows Interest in the Workers* brings the manager/employee relationship to the personal level. Managers who show interest in their workers understand that their people can make them or break them.

You can have the best facilities and equipment in the world, but if you do not have the right people in the right place, at the right time, and treat them right, you will lose the game.

The reason why business now have Human Resources department instead of Personnel Departments is to recognize that employees are people, not machines. A company's human assets are the most important assets they have.

Management Skills

In the end, good bosses with good personalities and good people skills still have to be good managers. One of the first thing employees expect is for their managers to have the *Ability to Solve Problems*.

While most people like to do their jobs on their own, when there is a problem they cannot handle they want help from management. If everything always ran smoothly, we would not need managers.

There is a simple progression of problem solving within an organization. Workers should be able to solve routine problems associated with their level of authority. First line supervisors should be able to handle problems that involve more decision making than their workers can handle, such as with budgets, customers complaints, suppliers, other departments, and upper management. Mid-level managers should be able to handle problems between lower level departments and upper level management. Top management should be able to handle all problems that come to them.

As we have seen, lack of managerial Accountability upsets many employees. People admire people who admit their mistakes and take responsibility when the mess up. People despise people who try to weasel out of the blame or worse yet, blame others for their shortcomings.

On the other side of the coin, taking credit for something someone else did falls in the same category as not taking responsibility. It is just as dishonest and despicable.

Of course, the follow up to problem solving skills is *Effective Decision Making Ability.* When employees have problem, they not only expect their bosses to be able to understand the problem, they want them to be able to do something about it. That's where decision making comes in.

We should not be foolish enough to think that our bosses should be able to make ever decision without making a few mistakes. No one is ppperfect and missstakes happen. See what I mean.

Not admitting mistakes and not trying to correct them is the problem with many managers. This brings us to looking at Effective Follow-Up Efforts.

There is a multitude of sequences in academic textbooks for the proper method of problem solving. Each one includes implementation, follow-up and revision.

The old saying that starts: "The best laid plans" is unquestionably true. Very few things go exactly as planned. Good managers keep up with what is going on around them and anticipate that changes will be necessary.

Employees get very frustrated when they know something is not working and no one does anything about it. They feel they are wasting their time and are even fearful that in the end, they will get the blame for being inefficient or ineffective.

At the outset, the ability to solve problems, make decisions and follow them up effectively requires *Good General and Job Specific Knowledge.* Employees want their bosses to be smart enough to handle their jobs. We can see in the *Jerk-Stories* that employees do not feel comfortable working for a boss that does not know the job.

Employees also want their overseers to understand life in general. They want their supervisors to understand the human condition. Book learning by itself does necessarily make a manager knowledgeable about what makes people behave the way they do. Understanding human needs and wants is vital to effective management of people.

As we have seen before, employees all want fair and equal treatment. Managers must provide *Impartial Evaluations.* In addition to being fair and impartial, evaluations should be constructive, not punitive. Unjust evaluations produce resentment and inefficiency.

Managers should never surprise their employees with a poor periodic evaluation. It should not be a game of waiting for an employee to hang his or her self for termination. Managers should address poor performance at the time it occurs.

Once more, we need to visit *People and Organizational Skills.* None of the other managerial skills will be effective without the ability to relate to the workers and understanding how to use their talents in the organization.

We need to stress repeatedly that good management and leadership is not only about managing time, money or things. Having enough money and things to do the job is important. However, not having enough of the right people, in the right place and at the right time is paramount.

Experience in a number of industries over a number of years shows that while technology changes from industry to industry, people are people no matter where they work. Good leadership is about people and helping them get the job done.

Finally, employees also need to know what they are to accomplish and how they should do it properly. Managers should not expect employees to know what the do not know. Management needs to *Provide Effective Training.*

That sounds simple. Yet, so many jerk-managers ask employees to do things without any training or guidance whatsoever. Then, when things go wrong they blame the employee. Without good training, it is like trying to find your way in the dark without someone shining a light on the way out. We have said before, good employees want to do a good job.

After analyzing these various jerk-stories, I think it is safe to conclude that it is necessary to have strong positive personal traits in order to form the foundation for good management and leadership. In common terms, we often refer to these traits as a person's personality.

What does it take to have a good positive personality? Regardless of your religion, or perhaps a lack of any belief in a Higher Power, the answer lies in understanding and following the Eight Beatitudes covered in the previous chapters. As I demonstrated in my book "Enjoy the Easy Life with Jesus," I think most modern psychologist would agree that they describe a roadmap for personal happiness and success in life. I think they are worth repeating

Blessed are the poor in spirit; theirs is the kingdom of heaven.

When Jesus referred to people who are poor in spirit, I don't think He meant that people should live in poverty. Although, I do believe that people who live in poverty can also be poor in spirit. History is full of stories of the lives of people who have lived in poverty and still found ways to help others even less fortunate.

I believe Jesus was telling us that all people are sinners and that we must understand that we cannot save ourselves by ourselves. Simply put, being poor in spirit means that we know that we need God and others in our life.

Self-righteousness and a better-than-thou attitude do not help a person to be poor in spirit. In social terms, narcissistic pride does not make for having many friends and does not add to one's happiness. In my experience, bragging, bravado and bigotry are usually cover-ups of low-self esteem. Think about this. How hard is it to have a conversation with a person who only talks about himself or herself? "Me, me, me" does not spell "us." People with good self-esteem don't have to put other people down.

Blessed are the Gentle

Some people think that being gentle is a sign of weakness. I prefer to think that the by being gentle Jesus meant we should be the strong silent type. We don't need to go around acting like we can lick the world. We don't have to control the world. All we need to do is respect ourselves and respect others. I think being gentle can be looked at in the sense of the old saying "you get more bees with honey." Hard-edged attitudes don't usually lead to very much respect from others.

Blessed those who mourn; they shall be comforted.

I think there are certainly times when we mourn the loss of someone we love. Sometimes through death and sometimes through divorce. We can mourn poor health and those precious things stolen from us by thieves and hurricanes. This is part of human nature. My wife and I, along with the rest of her family and friends, will surely mourn our daughter Carrie's early death for a long time to come.

When Jesus talks about those who mourn, he also means that we should mourn all the evil in the world. We should mourn the indignities people face in totalitarian societies. We should mourn human rights violations all over the world.

We should also mourn the fact that many of us simply ignore evil in others and evil in ourselves. We get used to evil situations and do nothing. We say, "What can one person do?"

One person can do wonders. Martin Luther changed religion forever and Martin Luther King changed America forever. Mother Theresa changed helping the poor forever.

People who mourn the evil around us are comforted and strengthened by standing up against that evil. If you fight against evil, you will not join evil. A guilt free mind is very comforting.

Blessed those who hunger and thirst for justice for they shall be satisfied.

It took me some time to realize that seeking justice and righteousness certainly does not mean being self-righteous. During my fallen-away days, I used to look at others whom I considered inconsiderate and unrighteous and I used to say: "I don't understand how people can act that way." What I was really saying to myself was that I thought that I was a better person than they were. I was disappointed by people and found fault in many of them. Yet, being "Mr. Wonderful" didn't make me happy.

When I learned to quit worrying about solving other people's problems and to concentrate on myself, I started accepting other people the way they are. I became much more open and accessible to others, and I enjoy the company of lots of people.

To me, hungering and thirsting for justice simple means trying to live a good God centered life. Live a righteous life and you will be seeking righteousness in the eyes of God. That's what counts. Never forget that everyone makes mistakes.

Blessed are the merciful: they shall have mercy.

How can we expect to be forgiven and receive mercy if we don't forgive and have mercy on others? Generally, we get back what we give out. When is the last time you asked someone to forgive you? Have you ever had to say, "I'm sorry?" I know I sure have, and I'm sure I will certainly have many occasions to ask for forgiveness from the people I love in the future.   Again, remember we all make mistakes and hurt people's feelings.

Showing mercy doesn't mean overlooking evil. Condoning evil is not being merciful. Someone who gives an alcoholic a drink of whiskey is not being merciful. Giving an alcoholic a drink of whiskey is being an enabler of evil.

If people continually do evil, we should avoid them. On the other hand, if they change we should give them the chance to regain our respect. However, we cannot make people change, only they can decide to change if the chose to do so.

Many people need our mercy, not our pity. If you give someone help out of pity, you are only easing your own conscience and are really just saying, "Thank God I don't have that person's problems."

Blessed are the pure in heart: they shall see God.

A pure heart does not envy. It does not deceive. It does not hate. It does not lust. It does not slander others. It does not have contempt. It does not covet.

A pure heart loves God and others. It is humble. It is meek. It is kind. It is gentle. It is charitable.

A pure heart frees a person to love. When we realize that God loves us just the way we are, then there is no end to the joy that we will find in others. The love of God is everywhere. All we have to do is open our hearts to God's unlimited love.

Blessed are the peacemakers, they shall be called sons of God.

Quick and easy, peacemakers are not troublemakers. Again, I don't mean that peaceful people are supposed to be whimps. Being peaceful simply means not being covetous and aggressive. We should be at peace with ourselves and with others. Peace within brings contentment with our station in life. Inner peace reduces worry about how we measure up to God and ourselves. The more faith I have, the more I love me, and the more peaceful I become.

Of course, there are times in everyone's life when doubt creeps in. Those are the times when I start to find fault in my actions and in others. Those are the times when I become self-righteous in order to cover up my own faults. Those are the times when I have trouble sleeping at night. Tossing and turning in bed is not good exercise. Losing inner peace is not fun.

Peace with others is what comes from having peace within. If we are contented with our own being, then we have no reason to find fault or be aggressive toward others. I truly believe that the source of all bigotry is low self-esteem, the lack of an inner peace and the need to feel better than other people. If someone is not as good as I am, then I must be better than they are.

Bigotry is just another form of self-righteousness. People at peace with themselves don't have to put other people down just to feel like they are better than others.

166

Blessed those persecuted in the cause of right: theirs is the kingdom of heaven

Sometimes it is not easy to stand up for your principles. Peer pressure can be great. Some people will ridicule you and some will ostracize you if you don't go along with their wishes to do evil.

There is no question that temptation is all around us. And, there is no question that, like me, most people will fall to temptation at times throughout life.

We all make mistakes. However, making the same mistake repeatedly is a serious problem, especially when we are hurting others by our harmful actions or inactions.

Do you have a management problem? If you are a manager, perhaps the stories in this book will help you avoid catching the destructive disease of *jerkism*.

References

Maslow, A. (1954), *Motivation and Personality*, New York, Harper & Row.

Matthew, Mark, Luke, and John (Last names unknown), (A long time ago), New Testament, Various places.

www.ingramcontent.com/pod-product-compliance
Lightning Source LLC
Chambersburg PA
CBHW051515170526
45165CB00002B/475